Other books by
Steve Dewey and Kevin Goodman

In Alien Heat: The Warminster Mystery Revisited
Steve Dewey and John Ries
Anomalist Books, ISBN: 978-1933665023

UFO Warminster: Cradle of Contact
Kevin Goodman and Steve Dewey
Fortean Words, ISBN: 978-1905723928

The Dead John Miscellany
John Ries, edited by Steve Dewey
CreateSpace, ISBN: 978-1500410667

Wiltshire Songs
Steve Dewey
watwo Kindle Edition

History of a Mystery
Fifty Years of the Warminster Thing

Steve Dewey
Kevin Goodman

An original publication of Swallowtail Books

History of a Mystery
Fifty Years of the Warminster Thing

Copyright © 2015
Steve Dewey and Kevin Goodman

ISBN-13: 978-0955119033
ISBN-10: 0955119030

http://www.ufo-warminster.co.uk

Cover design: Paul Vought

Swallowtail Books, Southampton, Hampshire, UK

CONTENTS

Warminster is a very nice town: everything belonging to it is solid and good.

William Cobbet, 'Rural Rides', 1826

Introduction

Two words: Remember Warminster? Put this question to a young ufologist, and the chances are you'll receive only a blank look in reply. Put the same question to older students of British UFO research, and you'll elicit one of two reactions: a mocking smile, followed by a dismissive retort; or a dreamy expression, followed, hopefully, by a long conversation full of memories of those long gone days and nights spent on the hills around the town, scanning the skies for unidentified flying objects (UFOs).

Before the Swinging Sixties, Warminster had never been famous for much. It is a small, unremarkable town in Wiltshire, in the south of England. At the time of writing this book, it has a population of around 18,000. It is an army town, home to the Land Warfare Centre (formerly the School of Infantry). Salisbury Plain, to the north of the town, is used for military manoeuvres and training, including live firing. In addition to the Army, the Royal Navy (Fleet Air Arm) and Royal Air Force also use the Plain, and joint services exercises sometimes take place.

Very few luminaries had come from the town, and very little had happened there.* However, in the 1960s,

---

* From the seventies onwards, the town began to generate notable musicians: various members of The Subhumans, Citizen Fish and the jazz saxophonist Andy Sheppard.

that was to change. Warminster was to become famous – notorious even – for its UFO sightings. These UFOs were described in the books of Arthur Shuttlewood, a local journalist. By the 1980s, the sightings had faded away, and memories of the events in the town were fading with them.

Over the last few years, however, there has been a resurgence of interest in Warminster's UFO mystery. *In Alien Heat: The Warminster Mystery Revisited*, by Steve Dewey and John Ries, was published in 2005, and Kevin Goodman's *UFO Warminster: Cradle of Contact* was published in 2006. Other ufological researchers have also begun to reappraise the events in Warminster; for example, David Clarke and Andy Roberts devote a chapter to Warminster in their *Flying Saucerers*.

What need is there, then, for another book? All the books ultimately rest on the primary texts: the books of Arthur Shuttlewood, and the local ufology magazines. Shuttlewood's books have been long out of print, and are only available to those who know how to search for them. Additionally, modern readers may find Shuttlewood's particular style of prose florid and dramatic. We thought a book was needed for those who had heard of the mystery, but knew little about it, a book with little commentary, criticism, or analysis of the phenomenon: a simple history of the mystery. This book, therefore, is historical in nature, and makes no comment on what did or did not happen. Readers interested in critical analyses of the Warminster mystery are directed at the books in the bibliography.

This book provides a short introduction to the phenomenon, and brings the story up to the present day.

We list very few of the sightings that Shuttlewood reports in his books; interested readers are directed to the encyclopaedic lists in John Hanson's *Haunted Skies* series, or to Ken Rogers' *The Warminster Triangle*.

The book begins with the eruption of the aural phenomenon in December 1964, and then describes the sightings that began in 1965 and continued through to the end of 1977. Although we do recount some of the stories that were reported, particularly at the beginning of the mystery, we concentrate mainly on the events and people that helped maintain the Warminster mystery in the national, and then the ufological consciousness; so, for example, we discuss the media interest in the 1960s, the publication of Shuttlewood's books, the opening and closing of Star House and the Fountain Centre, and so on.

The authors of this book are veterans of Warminster. We spent many nights on Cradle Hill during the 1970s, and have since researched the Warminster mystery in some depth. Kevin's experiences are documented in *UFO Warminster*; Steve's scepticism is expressed in *In Alien Heat*. As we noted above, however, *History of a Mystery* is not about analysis or criticism; and as both authors come from different sides of the fence, each has been able to check the natural tendency of the other towards a particular viewpoint in relation to the Warminster mystery.

There is no doubt that something happened in Warminster during the 1960s and 1970s. Whether you lean towards psychosocial or esoteric explanations, the evidence exists that something mysterious – spaceships, aliens, mass delusion, whatever – occurred. The mystery will never be fully explained to everybody's satisfaction. We have no doubt that the mystery will be revisited in future years, and we hope this book will provide a useful resource for future researchers as well as for those curious about the events in Warminster.

This, then, is the history of the almost forgotten mystery that began half a century ago.

And So Things Begin – 1965

In the early 1960s, Warminster was a quiet, unremarkable place. Arthur Shuttlewood, a journalist on the local paper, the *Warminster Journal*, had little to report except court cases, local meetings, minor crimes, and so on. For Shuttlewood, and for Warminster, things were about to change: a "sonic deluge broke with full fury" on some residents of the town. The reports of these sounds found their way to Shuttlewood, and then into the pages of the *Warminster Journal*.

Sounding Off

In the early hours of the morning of 25th of December, 1964, the first of these aural phenomena occurred. Here is how the *Warminster Journal* reported it in January 1965:

> Setting out for church at 6.30 on Christmas morning, a Bradley Road, Warminster, housewife heard a crackling noise from the direction of Bell Hill. At first she thought it was a lorry spreading grit on the hill. But the noise grew louder, came *over* her head and passed on across Ludlow Close.
>
> She will not let me use her name because she is afraid of being laughed at. The noise sounded like branches being pulled over gravel and there was a faint hum, it was quite loud but not above talking level. The sky was dark but brilliantly starlit and she could see nothing above her.

> Explanations have included: Static electricity caused by wet power lines, natural static electricity caused in certain weather conditions; a satellite:- and Father Christmas taking off!

> This shy lady would be glad to hear from anybody else who heard the noise or who could give some explanation. Her knees were knocking all the way to the church!

At roughly the same time, Roger Rump, Warminster's head postmaster, heard noises almost identical to those described by Mrs. Bye. His house was not far from Christ Church. He described:

> a terrific clatter ... As though the ... roof tiles were being rattled about and plucked off by some tremendous force. Then came a scrambling sound as if they were being ... loudly slammed back into place ... I could hear an odd humming tone. It was most unusual ... [it] lasted no more than a minute. (*The Warminster Mystery*, p.19)

Also on that Christmas morning – the time of this incident is not noted by Shuttlewood – over thirty soldiers at Knook camp, about four miles from Warminster, were rudely awoken by a loud noise. A sergeant told Shuttlewood that the sound was similar to that of a huge chimney stack being ripped from a roof and scattered in pieces across the whole of the camp. The guard was alerted, but nothing developed beyond the extraordinary sound. The soldiers were surprised but unable to explain the sound, although they claimed that it was unlike that of a conventional aircraft. (*The Warminster Mystery*, p.19)

It turned out that Mrs Bye and Mr Rump had not been the only witnesses to the 'sonic attacks'. When Shuttlewood's story about these strange sounds appeared in *The Warminster Journal*, other people began to report similar experiences from the same night.

Strange Noise At Warminster

SETTING off for church at 6.30 on Christmas morning, a Bradley Road, Warminster, housewife heard a crackling noise from the direction of Bell Hill. At first she thought it was a lorry spreading grit on the hill. But the noise grew louder, came *over* her head and passed on across Ludlow Close.

She will not let me use her name because she is afraid of being laughed at. The noise sounded like branches being pulled over gravel and there was a faint hum. It was quite loud but not above talking level. The sky was dark but brilliantly starlit and she could see nothing above her.

Explanations have included: static electricity caused by wet power lines; natural static electricity caused in certain weather conditions; a satellite; — and Father Christmas taking off!

This shy lady would be glad to hear from anybody else who heard the noise or who could give some explanation. Her knees were knocking all the way to church.

The first report in the *Warminster Journal* of the strange noises that were soon to be reported from all over the town.

13

Mildred Head had been woken at 1.45am on Christmas morning by what she described as a sound similar to twigs being dragged across the roof of her home. These sounds were followed by a different noise, like "giant hailstones pelting the roof". She had also been aware of a humming sound that grew louder, and then faded away. Her husband, who was deaf, had heard nothing, and continued sleeping. Wondering if there had been a storm, Mrs Head went to the window of her

SPACE SHIP OVERHEAD, HE CLAIMS

MYSTERIOUS crackling noises with a menacing humming at their centre have terrified a number of people in West Wiltshire over recent years.

Birds being killed while flying in the path of this phenomenon at Crockerton have been reported.

Mr. David Helton, "amateur scientist" living at Sutton-end Crockerton, near Warminister, is convinced there is only one possible explanation — a space ship from another planet is hovering over the county, preparing to make a landing.

Everything points to this, he claims, conclusion about the source of the weird noises heard by people in the area.

bedroom and looked outside, but found the sky clear and the ground dry.

These sonic phenomena were to continue into the first half of 1965. In March 1965, Mr and Mrs Brown reported that their roof had quivered under an "onrush" of the sounds. Mrs. Brown said their pet cat had vomited in various rooms of the house after the noise had died away. Pets, in particular, seemed to be frightened by these events. Shuttlewood noted that reports reached him of nervous and injured animals, both livestock and domestic pets. (See *The Warminster Mystery*, pp.26-31)

David C. Holton told Shuttlewood of a flock of birds that had been killed in flight in February, 1965. This occurred at Five Ash Lane, on the southern outskirts of Warminster. Holton claimed to have examined the birds shortly after they had died. He believed the birds had been killed by sound waves, possibly caused by *the Thing*, as the UFO phenomenon around Warminster was to become known.

Ted and Gwen Davies lived in Crockerton, a village only two miles south of Warminster, and south of Five Ash Lane, where Holton's birds had been killed. On the morning of Thursday, 25th March 1965, while they were eating breakfast, they both heard what sounded like the flapping of birds' wings, and a crackling noise around their chimney. This was followed by a metallic grinding sound. "Our rafters shook and our windows rattled", Mrs. Davies said, "[like] there was a gale force wind". Both went outside, but there was no sign of any birds; the sky was clear, and the morning was still.

Late on the evening of 28th March, 1965, Eric Payne was returning to Warminster on foot after seeing his girlfriend safely home in Sutton Veny. Near Bishopstrow he heard a whistling noise that then developed into a loud buzzing. He described the noise as "A gigantic tin can with huge nuts and bolts inside it, rattling overhead". In spring 1965, Mr and Mrs Marson were to experience the noise on three occasions, two of these events happening within a short space of time on the same night. Mrs Marson said: "It was a great bouncing and bumping noise over our heads. As though a load of stones was being tipped against the roof and the back wall of the bungalow". Her husband said: "It seemed as if tons of coal were being emptied from sacks and sent tumbling all over the place. It all began with an electric crackling". Mr and Mrs Marson also reported that a high-pitched droning was also evident. They inspected the area outside their house the following morning, expecting to find debris, but found nothing out of the ordinary. A similar event occurred on the night of June 1st 1965. Mrs. Marson reported to Shuttlewood that she heard a loud humming noise, followed by bumping sounds. Mrs Marson later saw a brilliant white light which lit their bedroom with such intensity "it seemed like day time".

Lights in the Sky

Mrs Marson's sighting reminds us that although the Thing had arrived in Warminster as an aural phenomenon, it quickly changed to a visual phenomenon.

Most Warminster residents would only have learned of the visual nature of the Thing through a report in the *Warminster Journal* of a UFO seen by the wife of the vicar of Heytesbury, Mrs. Patricia Phillips. She had phoned

Arthur Shuttlewood to inform him of a cigar-shaped glow that she could see hanging in the sky. She observed the object for over twenty-five minutes, certain that it did not change position during this time. She told Shuttlewood that there was a dark circular patch at the base of the object. It had a ring around the lower end. After a while the object seemed to grow shorter, as if it was turning on its axis. It then dis-appeared. Her 12-year old son, Nigel, watched the object through a pair of child's binoculars, and was able to draw a picture of the object afterwards. The object was also seen by Mrs Phillips' husband, their three children, and a visitor. This sighting was soon confirmed as the first mass sighting. After the story had been published in the *Journal*, further witnesses came forward with stories that appeared to corroborate Mrs Phillips' story. The UFO was also seen, these stories suggested, by Warminster residents Mr and Mrs Horlock, who described the UFO as "Twin red-hot pokers hanging downwards, one on top of the other, with a black space in between"*; and by seventeen people swimming or fishing at Shearwater, a lake on the Longleat Estate near Warminster. One of the Shearwater witnesses told Shuttlewood "It was obviously huge, but very high up". Shuttlewood notes in his book, *The Warminster Mystery*, that the "evidence came in before any news of this extraordinary night vision had been published". (pp. 37-39)

Soon, more sightings were being reported. The evening of the 19th June was humid, and Mrs. Kathleen Penton was opening an upstairs window when she saw:

---

* Mrs Horlock saw another, similar, UFO at a later date.

this shining thing going along sideways in the sky, from right to left. Porthole type windows ran the entire length of it. It glided slowly in front of the downs… it was the size of a whole bedroom wall… It was very much like a train carriage, only with rounded ends to it. It did not travel lengthways, but was gently gilding sideways. (*The Warminster Mystery*, pp.37-39)

Even though people had started seeing UFOs, the noises still continued. The most spectacular of these events occurred on 17th August, 1965, when a large explosion rocked houses on the Boreham Field housing estate. Described as "a huge blast! A whole series of jolts and explosions ... the biggest explosion I have ever heard" that resulted in "a monstrous orange flame in the sky ... shaped like an electric bulb". Windows in two houses were broken, but this was the only damage caused by the "explosion".

Seeking possible causes for the explosion, Shuttlewood talked to officials at the nearby School of Infantry and Battlesbury Barracks, and at local military airfields. All denied responsibility. Explanations suggested to Shuttlewood for the events that night included thunderbolts and meteorites, but these he "wrote off as highly improbable". Full details of the events that evening are provided on pp.65-68 of *The Warminster Mystery*.

The Thing Goes National

The report of the sighting made in Heytesbury by Mrs Phillips, described above, first appeared in the *Warminster Journal* of the 4th of June. Shuttlewood, however, had access to popular daily and weekly newspapers. He visited the Phillips household soon after the sighting, and copied the sketch, made by Mrs

Phillips' son, of the UFO they had seen. Shuttlewood wrote an article to accompany the sketch, and sold the story to the *News of the World*, who printed it on the 6th of June, 1965. Shuttlewood's access to mainstream newspapers was to prove pivotal in proselytizing the Warminster phenomena. Also to prove pivotal were local personalities, ufological personalities, and the hunger of the media for novelty. To these, we shall now turn.

Things Continue
Media and Personalities

The Warminster mystery did not long remain parochial, known only to curious and interested locals. It quickly became known nationally and then internationally. There were many reasons why this happened: Shuttlewood's access to the media, the interest of ufological groups, the media's interest in stories of a paranormal nature, and the involvement of various personalities, including Shuttlewood himself. His role within the emerging story of the Thing is complex, and has been discussed in depth in *In Alien Heat*. It is not within the scope of this book to provide an analysis of how Shuttlewood might have helped shape the mystery. Shuttlewood is, however, possibly the most important personality in the Warminster mystery, so a brief outline of his role in the development of the mystery and his place in Warminster society begins this chapter.

Arthur Shuttlewood

When the Thing first began to make a noise and to light up the skies around Warminster, Shuttlewood was 44 years old, and had been writing for the *Warminster Journal* for many years. He was born in Chelmsford, Essex, in 1920, and moved to Warminster in 1940. He worked as a reporter, first for the *Wiltshire Times*, then for *The Warminster Journal*, from the early 1950s. Before becoming a journalist, Shuttlewood had been a member of the Grenadier Guards and the Air Ministry Constabulary, and a councillor on Warminster Urban District Council. He died in Warminster in 1996.

Shuttlewood always proclaimed his hard-headedness and scepticism, stating "I am not easily fooled. I dare not be. I have built my reputation as a journalist on the bedrock of integrity". (*Warnings From Flying Friends*, p.38)

Shuttlewood's position as a journalist provided him access to many witnesses to the Thing; he therefore became the primary source of information about the phenomenon. He was also the first to hear any stories of strange events occurring around the town. Inevitably, when UFO investigators or reporters came to Warminster, the person to whom they were directed was Shuttlewood. His charm won over many journalists, and even sceptical ufologists such as John Rimmer of *Magonia*. Everybody who met Shuttlewood was, it seems, struck by his sincerity, tenacity and rustic charm. John Rimmer reflects on Shuttlewood's role in an article "Warminster Revisited - Some Personal Observations", in the *Merseyside UFO Bulletin* (Vol. 2, No. 5, September - October 1969). Rimmer thought it unlikely that Shuttlewood had deliberately created the mystery; neither did he believe that Shuttlewood deliberately exaggerated the sightings he reported in his books. For Rimmer, Shuttlewood was simply a reporter, writing in a style that came naturally to him.

Eventually, Shuttlewood was to become a guru to the ufological fraternity that frequented the hills around Warminster; not only because of his charisma, but also through his position as the favoured intermediary between the esoteric and the mundane, and his increasing comfort in the language of the mystic and the visionary. We shall investigate these facets of his personality in later chapters.

For now, however, we need to explain Shuttlewood's relationship to the media, particularly to newspapers. As we saw in the previous chapter, Shuttlewood had managed to sell the story of the Phillip's sighting to a national newspaper, *The News of the World*. How could a reporter on a local newspaper get a story into a national?

As a correspondent to Steve Dewey noted when he was writing *In Alien Heat*, "no-one ever made a fortune out of working for a local paper". The correspondent – we'll call him Mr A – began working for the *Wiltshire Times* at about the same time as Arthur Shuttlewood. Mr A remembers being paid 54 shillings – £2.70 – a week, but had been paid £4 a week as a casual farm labourer the year before. There was no overtime paid, even though journalists did a lot of work in the evenings and also worked most Saturdays. Mr A remembers, though, that he did get a half-day's leave on a Friday – unless, of course, there was something newsworthy happening.

Shuttlewood's task was to cover the Warminster area for the *Wiltshire Times*. The best way to supplement income as a journalist on a provincial or local newspaper was to become a local correspondent for a national newspaper. Shuttlewood signed up as the local correspondent for most of the national and popular daily and Sunday papers. If something happened in the local correspondent's area for which a national paper required help, the national would call on the local correspondent to do research for which an agreed fee would be paid. The local correspondent would also be responsible for coverage of local stories, and would be paid either an agreed fee, or lineage. Lineage was payment by the word or line – say 2p a word, or 10p a line.

Shuttlewood could, therefore, have made as much out of lineage – and any expenses he charged – as he could have from his salary "even without exerting himself", as Mr A notes. A story such as the Warminster Thing – whether real or not, given the interest national newspapers had (and still have) in paranormal stories – could, at its peak, have provided Shuttlewood a substantial additional income. An exclusive story for a national, especially with a photograph, would be worth twice the usual fee, and for a paper like the *Sunday Mirror* might have provided a month's salary.

None of this is meant to imply that Shuttlewood himself invented the Thing solely to make money. The media interest in the Warminster mystery was brief, while the phenomenon itself – and Shuttlewood's interest and part in it – continue for at least another ten years. As a professional journalist, and a local correspondent to national papers, it would have been sensible for Shuttlewood to attempt to make extra money using his craft as a reporter during the brief period of intense media interest in the mystery. Shuttlewood, like many people, had a wife and family to support. Who can blame him for going for the lineage, exclusives and expenses?

Arthur Shuttlewood, 1920-1996

David Holton's Interest in Things

David Holton is a name that appears often in Shuttlewood's *The Warminster Mystery*. Holton's role in the mystery is described and examined in detail in *In Alien Heat*. It is worth noting here, though, that the source of many of the early stories reported to Shuttlewood was David Holton. It was Holton who told Shuttlewood the dramatic story about the pigeons that had died at Five Ash Lane.

Holton lived in the village of Crockerton, about two miles out of Warminster. He practiced surgical chiropody, but was also a naturalist, amateur geologist, homeopathic practitioner and medical herbalist.

Holton was among the first to suggest that the strange sounds around Warminster were caused by alien space-ships; Shuttlewood claimed that Holton had created a file of reports of the noises in the area. Holton was also among the first to write letters to the *Warminster Journal*, theorising about the causes of the noises. As early as the 15th January 1965, a letter from Holton was printed in the *Journal* in which he claimed that the noises were not unusual, had been reported around Warminster before, and also reported from other parts of the globe. Holton later appeared on the TV program *In the News*, where he said that the noises were connected to spaceships, and that those spaceships were preparing to land in Wiltshire.

The pages of the *Journal* were to become lively with correspondence about the Thing in the first few months of 1965. Holton was very active at this time, sending letters that contained his own ideas about the Thing, or that rebutted the ideas of other letter-writers.

Holton's involvement in the Warminster mystery was, however, surprisingly brief – Holton is often cited in the early chapters of *The Warminster Mystery*, but his name is mentioned much less after August 1965. The reasons for Holton's withdrawal from the mystery we will investigate in a later chapter. Nonetheless, for the short time he was involved, Holton was a busy actor in the mystery.

Media Interest in Things

Shuttlewood would, anyway, have had no market for his stories if the media, particularly the newspapers, didn't have a continuing interest in stories of the paranormal. For example, in 2014 there have been reports of Black-eyed Children, mysterious explosions and Alien Big Cats. Given that he was already a local correspondent to national newspapers, Shuttlewood was able, at least in the early days of the mystery, to find a ready outlet for his stories.

Television had already shown an interest in the Thing, with local news reports and, as noted above, Holton's appearance on a television magazine programme. Television was about lend its crowd-pulling powers to the Warminster myster. Emlyn Rees, who was head of the local Chamber of Commerce, suggested that a public meeting be held on Friday, 27th of August to discuss the Thing. The date of the meeting was close to the August Bank Holiday (which would have been Monday, 30th August).

Both television and Fleet Street were eager to cover the meeting – the Phillips sighting of June 3rd had by then been reported in the *Daily Mirror* and *The News of the World*. It should also be noted that, in Britain, Parliament goes into recess during the summer; stories other than the political are sucked into the news vacuum. These are often referred to as 'silly-season stories'. For the media, the Warminster mystery was very much a silly-season story, with most mainstream media coverage appearing between June and September of 1965.

The meeting was to provide little new information about the Thing. Even Shuttlewood thought the meeting 'fruitless'. Reports about the meeting did, however, have at least one affect; they informed and attracted the curious, who flocked to Warminster. Over the August Bank Holiday weekend the population of Warminster, at that time only 11,000, increased to over 18,000. The sceptical Christopher Evans noted that:

> If there were any doubts about the pulling powers of the saucers … the local tradesmen must soon have had their minds put to rest … A vast surge of curiosity seekers descended on Warminster … bleeding the souvenir shops dry and bringing to the point of collapse the town's modest catering establishments. (Christopher Evans, *Cults of Unreason*, p.178)

Ufology's Interest in Things

Whatever British ufology now makes of the Warminster mystery, and whatever it made of it after the first year of excitement, it was, *during* 1965, the biggest thing ever to happen in British ufology. Whether the media interest in the Thing led to ufological interest, or whether the Thing found its way to ufological groups through the grape-

'THE THING' STARTS CASH TILLS RINGING

A NEW noise was heard in Warminster yesterday—the merry tinkling of cash registers.

Tourists from all over the country are pouring into the Wiltshire town (population 11,000) to go Thing-spotting.

Nobody knows what The Thing is. But the townsfolk of Warminster say it is responsible for the fireball in the sky, the weird sounds and other strange happenings reported in the district over the past two years.

'As good as Loch Ness'

And last night there was no room at any Warminster inn. At the Anchor Hotel, Scots landlord Hugh McLaren, 53, said: "This could do us as much good as the Loch Ness monster did for Scotland."

Over at the Weymouth Arms, Mr. Pat Kelly, 46, secretary of the local licensed Victuallers' Association said: "The Thing could keep our season going right through the winter."

The Big Rush to Warminster follows Friday night's public meeting at the town hall at which it was decided to set up a Thing observation post on the Downs.

Said council chairman, Mr. Emlyn Rees, who organised the meeting : "One man from London has already volunteered to man the post at weekends. We might even get the Observer Corps in on it."

The Londoners will join local volunteers equipped with tape recorders, cameras and binoculars to record any odd sight or sound.

But even townsfolk who are welcoming the tourists with open arms are maintaining a healthy cynicism.

Said retired travel agent Joe Brownell, 74, member of the town's Tourist Committee : "If these visitors expect to see the Thing I think they will be disappointed."

vine is uncertain. What is certain, however, is that one of the earliest UFO sightings – unreported in the *Journal*, but described in *The Warminster Mystery* – was first reported to a ufology group, the Fleet Street UFO Group, who then forwarded the details to Shuttlewood. (See *The Warminster Mystery*, pp.34-35 for the description of this sighting).

Flying Saucer Review (*FSR*) became aware of the Thing soon after it had crashed and banged its way into the skies above Warminster. *FSR* of July-August 1965 (Vol. 11, No. 4) contained an article by Charles Bowen and Gordon Creighton, 'The Warminster Phenomenon', that provided a description of the mystery, particularly the noises; noted the research of David Holton; and reported one of the earliest UFO sightings, that of June 1965. *FSR* was taking the Warminster phenomenon seriously. Indeed, it is difficult to see how it could have done otherwise, given that Gordon Creighton, editor of *FSR*, had been one of those writing to *The Warminster Journal* suggesting an extra-terrestrial solution to the vexing problem of the noises.

Examination of Shuttlewood's books reveals that many ufologists who were prominent at the time or were to achieve later prominence became involved in the Warminster mystery. As we have seen, Creighton was among the first to write to the *Journal*. John Cleary-Baker, evaluating officer and secretary of the British UFO Research Association (BUFORA), also wrote a letter to the *Warminster Journal*, requesting information for an article he was writing for the BUFORA journal. G. G. Doel, then chairman of BUFORA, and John Cleary-

Baker were both on the panel at the Warminster Town Hall meeting described in the previous section.

The euphoria, excitement, criticism and arguments caused by the events in Warminster in many ways defined British ufology, both then and now.

Selling Stories, Telling Stories

The scene, then, had been set. The media, always receptive to stories of a paranormal, pseudoscientific or just plain odd nature had found in the Warminster mystery the perfect space- and time-filler for the silly season. Shuttlewood and others, such as David Holton, were providing reports and narratives that were taken up by the media. Shuttlewood himself, as a reporter on the *Warminster Journal*, and as a local correspondent for national newspapers, had access to both witness reports and outlets for those reports. Ufological groups and researchers such as *FSR* and BUFORA soon became involved. The Warminster mystery thus quickly became a *legitimate* mystery; the national media and ufological groups provided that legitimacy. It also continued to be an *unsolved* mystery, as claims that the sounds and lights were caused by alien spaceships were – and continue to be – unresolved.

If Warminster had provided no new mysteries after the silly season, the excitement – and the lights and sounds that went with it – might soon have faded away. But there were twists to come, enough to power the developing narrative for the next ten years. By the end of summer, 1965, the Warminster mystery was big.

It was about to become bigger.

Things Continue
Through the End of '65

As we have previously described, something strange happened in Warminster in early 1965. Reports of strange sounds were followed by more phenomena, both audio and visual, each instance of which came to be called *the Thing*: "we saw a thing in the sky", "we heard some *thing* making a noise". By the middle of 1965, reports of the Thing in various media had generated enough interest to encourage the head of the local chamber of commerce to arrange a meeting about it at the Town Hall. The meeting, covered in newspapers and on local television news, had in turn encouraged interested visitors to Warminster over the Bank Holiday weekend. The Warminster mystery was to continue for another ten years after that. What could keep ufologists and the curious coming to Warminster? What would continue to stimulate interest? A sighting of the Thing, clearly photographed in daylight, would undoubtedly help. And it did.

The Faulkner Photograph

On the evening of the 29th of August, 1965, Gordon Faulkner stepped outside his house and closed the front door. He was on his way to his mother's house, taking with him a camera that his sister had asked to borrow.

He suddenly became aware of something "flying fast and low over the south of the town. Faulkner could see that the shape of the object was unusual; the object made no noise. He grabbed the camera he had been taking to his sister, and pointed it at the craft, but it was travelling too fast for him to follow. Instead, he focused some way ahead of the object and pressed the shutter release as it entered the viewfinder. Faulkner thought it unlikely he had captured anything and so was "amazed" when he saw the print. (*The Warminster Mystery*, p.61)

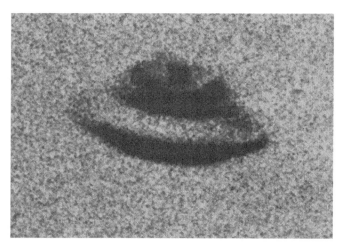

The Faulkner Photograph
This is the crop and enlargement usually shown in books

Faulkner sent a copy of the print with a letter describing the sighting to the *Warminster Journal*; the letter appeared in the 'Letters to the Editor' column in the Friday, 10th September, edition of the *Journal*. Shuttlewood, who had become aware of the picture and accompanying story, had written an article for the *Daily Mirror* that was also published on the same day.

The photograph shows a small object in the sky over Warminster. The enlargement, which is the image usually reproduced in UFO books, shows a typical disc-shaped object, with a domed top. It is difficult to make out details on the object, as the enlargement is very grainy.

Shuttlewood had travelled to London to ensure the story made the pages of the *Daily Mirror*. Members of staff to whom he showed the photograph were sceptical. Aerospace reporter Peter Harris said to Shuttlewood, "this picture does not convince me". Arthur Smith, science reporter, stated that "it is one of the best photographs ever taken, but the lack of any knowledge of the size or distance renders its scientific value to nil". He pointed out that other pictures like it were usually fakes. Smith added: "The Warminster picture is in a different category - but there is no way of solving its mystery". Despite this scepticism, the *Daily Mirror* printed the article. (*The Warminster Mystery*, p.62)

Although very few sightings of the Thing occurred during daylight hours – most sightings were at night, and were simply lights in the sky – the Thing as represented in Faulkner's photograph has become emblematic. Of all the photographs taken of the Warminster Thing, this one is the "best", and has been reproduced the most often.

Shuttlewood's Conversion

As we noted in the previous chapter, Shuttlewood declared that he was not easily fooled, and had built his journalistic reputation "on the bedrock of integrity". He claims to have maintained a kind of hard-headed journalistic scepticism about the mystery, until his own UFO sighting, on 28th September 1965. With that sighting, he became the 199th witness to anomalous phenomena around Warminster. Note the last statement: one hundred and ninety-nine witnesses, since the beginning of 1965; that is, in nine months there had been roughly one witness to strangeness every day. No wonder the Warminster mystery was so very exciting. By late August of 1965, Shuttlewood notes in *The Warminster Mystery* (p.65), he was already filling his eighth notebook relating to the local phenomena.

What did Shuttlewood see that changed his views? He told a television interviewer for the BBC TV programme *Pie in the Sky*, which was broadcast in April 1966, that the event would "always be indelible on my mind". At 3.42pm on September 28th, 1965, Shuttlewood was going up the stairs in his home to collect some notes for a story he was writing. At one of the windows, his attention "was arrested by this huge cigar shape in the sky". Shuttlewood continued:

> Now, had I normally been walking underneath that, I am sure that it would have assumed the proportions of nothing more than a dense white cloud. But from the angle of vision I had from the top of the house I could see a peculiar hump, a yellow or burnished amber protrusion from the top. And I'd never seen anything like this in my entire life. It was nine months since this thing started. I honestly don't think that I'd been conditioned to all that extent, although I've lived within the vortex or the centre of this mystery – and let's face it, it is a mystery. But I wasn't convinced, despite the high calibre of witnesses, that this thing existed. But I saw this with my own eyes.

Shuttlewood hurried to get his cine camera. He trained the camera on the object, which was gliding, "a silent gentle giant in the sky" over Colloway Clump, to the northwest. The camera then began to jump about in his hands, and he felt "sharp prickling needles" down his right-hand side, including his hand, wrist, and face. Shuttlewood noted that his "eye watered for two months afterward".

The malfunction in the cine camera, and the prickling in his body, proved to Shuttlewood that "whoever, or whatever was on board", could see him and his camera, and had used a "kind of concentrated force-field" in a deliberate attempt to affect the camera. "And, of course," Shuttlewood said, "they succeeded... Nothing developed from 25 feet of film, except an eight feet portion that had burnt right through. That's all I had on my camera".

Although there is some evidence that Shuttlewood already harboured belief in various paranormal phenomena prior to the Warminster mystery, it was this sighting, Shuttlewood claimed in both this interview and in *The Warminster Mystery,* that converted him to acceptance of the Thing as evidence of extraterrestrial spacecraft. It is a moot point whether Shuttlewood's own conversion to the cause fanned the flames of the phenomenon. Books such as John Spencer's *UFO Encyclopaedia*, (London, Headline: 1991) note that "for around a decade [Warminster] was to remain the British centre of Ufology, largely due to the diligent efforts of a local devotee, Arthur Shuttlewood" (p.318); and there is no doubt that when Shuttlewood became a skywatcher himself, he began to generate UFO reports of his own.

However, it should also not be forgotten that, for many months, Shuttlewood had only been a reporter of the phenomenon. There had been many others who had also fanned the flames.

Shuttlewood Gets a Call

What wasn't reported in *The Warminster Journal* – despite it obviously being big news – was the series of contacts Shuttlewood had with aliens. The wider ufological college knew little about these contacts until *The Warminster Mystery* was published in 1967. Shuttlewood notes in that book that he had discussed these contacts only with his close circle of friends.

The aliens that contacted Shuttlewood were from the planet Aenstria. The Aenstrians telephoned Shuttlewood from a telephone box in Boreham Fields, in Warminster. Boreham Fields is very close to the Army's barracks, and to the area where the mysterious explosion had occurred earlier in the year. Shuttlewood was contacted by three Aenstrians: Caellsan, a senior spacecraft commander; Traellison, the Queen of Aenstria; and Selorik, the English interpreter for Aenstria. All contact with Shuttlewood was via the phone. It appears that Selorik was surplus to requirements, as Traellison spoke directly to Shuttlewood: "Shrewd, sweet, and sensible. That is how I view Traellison, judging from her voice and the messages she relayed to me". (*The Warminster Mystery*, p.202) Perhaps "Queen" was some kind of error in translation or understanding; it seems to us rather short-sighted to transport the head of the planet-wide system of government across the vast and undoubtedly dangerous reaches of space.

Despite some reservations, Shuttlewood believed the contacts to be hoaxes. Shuttlewood claims he was tempted to omit the revelations of the Aenstrians from *The Warminster Mystery*. However, those friends with whom he had discussed the contacts thought the information relayed by these 'hoaxers' fascinating, and were to persuade Shuttlewood to add an appendix about the contacts to his book. While continuing to suspect hoaxers had perpetrated the phone calls, he nonetheless thought the information passed to him had been 'sensible'.

This 'sensible' information translates, in *The Warminster Mystery*, to eleven or twelve pages of homilies and New Age wisdom. (The core of it is on pp.188-203) The Aenstrians had contacted Shuttlewood because he was a journalist, and they hoped he could use his position to pass on their messages to the "councils" of our planet, which they called a 'cantel'. It is interesting that the only word that the Aenstrians do not translate is "cantel", which is simply an anagram of "planet" with the "p" replaced with a "c".

The messages relayed by the Aenstrians were those we have come to expect from extra-terrestrials, especially aliens that visited in the 1960s. After the usual caveat that space-folk were not empowered to interfere in the political processes of Earth, the Aenstrians warned of:

- Ecological disasters: diseases caused by the disposal of toxic wastes in the oceans, pollution caused by fertilisers and pesticides, the pollution of the atmosphere with vehicle exhausts, and our bodies with bad food. The Aenstrians were particularly worried about pollution of the water supplies, and were already engaged in remedial work to remove "harmful piles of waste atomic products from seabeds and take them away for aerial processing".

- Particular forms of scientific and military experiment. Humans should be particularly careful with atomic power, they said as:

  man could so easily topple headlong over the verge of safety into utter oblivion, from sanity to suicidal madness. The envelope of our Earth would, if we did not exert great care, ignite from end to end in a blazing inferno.

  This would destroy the "creative" system of our planet, disrupt the entire solar system, and even affect Aenstria itself. Aenstria would be affected "because the atmosphere beyond our own cantel is desperately thin".

- Excess radiation in our skies, and the resultant mutations this might cause,

The Aenstrians were, of course, far in advance of us, spiritually, politically and technologically. They lived to a ripe old age and suffered little sickness; Traellison was already 450 years old, and was considered quite young on Aenstria.

Traellison urged humankind to return to simpler, more spiritual ways. There were too many egotists in power, and "political danger within". Humankind "is off balance and off-key, out of step with the desired pattern of life predestined for us at the beginning of Man's creation". Yes, the Aenstrians did say "man's creation". Not only were they monarchists, but they appeared to be creationists as well. The Aenstrians told Shuttlewood

that "Man was created in individual mould...not des-
cended from fish or apes". Traellison said that humans
suffered unnecessarily with excessive mental illness and
physical distress; and that this was caused by the "hectic
pace of modernised life "and "the decided weakening of
moral fibre and religious supplication". Traellison's
remedy was a complete and radical change in our mode
of living; only then could we be free of depression and
tragedy. Corruption and greed are bad. Financial gain
and commercial endeavour are only valid "when divor-
ced from debasing motives". And Traellison noted that
"venereal and other diseases, abortion, and families split
asunder were the consequence of our moral laxity". If
only, it seems, we had listened to the "great Teacher ...
sent to Earth 2,000 ... years ago".

We wonder why, if *The Warminster Journal* was not an
adequate outlet for Shuttlewood's contactee stories,
Shuttle-wood did not avail himself of the national
papers that had been eager for his UFO reports. Perhaps
Shuttlewood's belief that the calls had been hoaxes
restrained him. Nonetheless, it was a tale he was telling
on the ufological lecture circuit. Members of the
Merseyside UFO Research Group attended the BUFORA
Northern Conference at Bradford on 10 September 1966,
at which Shuttlewood was the main speaker. John
Harney wrote a review of this lecture, which was published in the October 1966 issue of the *MUFORG Bulletin*;
in the review, Harney notes that "the spacemen have
taken to ringing Shuttlewood up on the telephone".

Mystery Men, and Sightings Continue

Given the recently televised town-hall meeting, Faulkner's photograph, and Shuttlewood's conversion, it is unsurprising that sightings and other mysterious events continued to be reported to Shuttlewood. The local population had been primed for mystery, and skywatchers were visiting the hills around the town.

In October, reports began to filter through to Shuttlewood of 'mystery men' in the Warminster area. One such report concerned a man who collapsed in Silver Street. Notably – at least to Shuttlewood – although the morning had been cold the man had been dressed only in light trousers and a thin shirt. Witnesses came forward to confirm they had seen the same man earlier on the Bath road, walking as if drunk. The mysterious stranger was taken to the local Warminster Hospital where he stayed unconscious for over four hours. Despite questioning by the police and hospital staff, he refused to say where he had come from, or why he was in such a state. He discharged himself from hospital two days later. Shuttlewood wondered, in *The Warminster Mystery*, if the man might somehow have been connected to the Thing, or even be one of its occupants. (*The Warminster Mystery*, pp.127-128)

On the 30th October, a school boy, Alan Ford, sighted a flying object between Norridge Wood and Cley Hill, to the north-west of Warminster. It appeared to turn back in its course, and was like "a fried egg – a white disc with a golden dome to it. It was quite big, even from a distance. I'm sure other people would have seen".

The following day there was a sighting over Shearwater Lake, on the Longleat Estate. Two bright, round objects were seen converging overhead. After tilting slightly towards each other, the witnesses reported that the objects remained stationary for nearly an hour. As the witnesses left the scene in a car, the two passengers sitting in the back of the car saw the objects descend towards the surface of the lake. The witnesses admitted to being frightened by what they'd seen, and had left the area quickly.

Even though UFO *sightings* were now the dominant phenomenon in the Warminster mystery, there was still the occasional report of unidentified noises. On December 3rd, Eva Goodwin told Shuttlewood that she had been awakened by "The crashing of pebbles on the roof "; this was followed by a thunderous roar, and a high pitched droning. When she turned on the light, it seemed as if the walls and ceiling were vibrating wildly. In panic, she fled the room, only to find the remaining rooms in the house were affected by this phenomenon.

Sightings continued on into December, 1965. Early on the morning of the 20th, Eva Robinson told Shuttlewood that she had seen a large, silver cigar, not unlike a Zeppelin, travelling silently in the sky. She was adamant that it had not been a balloon. (The sightings are reported in *The Warminster Mystery*, pp.137-142.)

One Year On

Eva Robinson's sighting of late December reminds us that the excitement, the thrill, the wonder, the awe – the Warminster mystery – had now been continuing for nearly a year. In that time there had been meetings, media and ufologists in the town, all seeking confirmation that the Warminster mystery was a mystery that involved spaceships and aliens. The mystery now had a head of steam. It had accelerated throughout the year, and the pace of sightings and wonders was like an express train. The train did, however, begin to slow. Although media interest was to decrease, it would still continue – a result, in part, of Shuttlewood's role as a local correspondent.

Now, however – because of the involvement of the media and ufological groups – people with an interest in UFOs were aware of the mystery. Warminster became a site for dedicated skywatchers and ufological tourists. Cradle Hill, to the north-east of Warminster, became the favoured skywatching location. The skywatchers and the tourists began to have their own experiences – to see, feel and hear their own Things – and generated reports that added to the sightings made by the local population. The Warminster mystery had become, for the next decade or so, self-sustaining.

Cradle Hill, with the copse on the brow of the hill

The Flap Continues – 1966

As we move into 1966, we leave behind the "hysterical" period of the Warminster mystery. Never again would media interest in the Thing be as intense as it had been in 1965. Nonetheless, that interest would continue, at least in part because of Shuttlewood's role as a local correspondent for national and regional newspapers. Television documentaries about UFOs would also continue to feature Warminster. The *Warminster Journal* would, however, cease to carry stories about the Thing; possibly because, as Ray Shorto, editor of the *Journal* noted in a review of *In Alien Heat*, Charles Mills, Shuttlewood's editor and owner of the *Journal* at that time, thought the Warminster mystery "a whole load of rubbish and did not want the *Journal* to be the laughing stock of the town." ('A Return to the Days of the Mysterious UFOs', *Warminster Journal*, 28th December, 2006. Ray Shorto is the grandson of Charles Mills.)

The Reports Continue

Even without the exposure the *Journal* once provided, Things continued to be seen throughout 1966. For example, at the beginning of the year:

- Nicholas Gill saw three bright crimson balls flying north to south overhead at 9.00pm, on January 3rd, spaced at regular intervals, silent, and travelling below the clouds. When they were directly above him, their shape was circular; they then changed to an egg shape as they travelled away towards the horizon.

- Three young people reported a series of white lights, at 8.55pm on the 17th January. Some of these seemed to "pop out" as the witnesses watched them; the remaining objects changed course several times during the sighting.

- Mrs. E. Noakes reported a sighting, from her home in the village of Upton Scudamore, of a huge silvery cigar gliding without noise over her head in the direction of Cradle Hill. The object was surrounded by a bright aura or halo. Her sons and daughters confirmed the sighting. (*The Warminster Mystery*, p.145)

In early February, Shuttlewood noted an "unnatural calm". Things seemed to be tailing off. (*The Warminster Mystery*, p.161) Was it possible that people were becoming wary of reporting sightings for fear of ridicule? It is a possibility – but as the remainder of 1966 was to become active again, it is possible that February was a temporary blip. Perhaps it was the weather – February was one of the wettest up until that time over England and Wales.

Pie in the Sky

If the *Warminster Journal* was no longer able to provide the stories that would excite interest in the Thing, other sources still could. If some local residents feared ridicule, there would continue to be, however irregularly, media events that would legitimise their experiences. As we alluded to in the introductory paragraphs to this chapter, media interest in the Thing had tailed off, but had not stopped entirely. On the 1st of April, 1966, the BBC broadcast to its South and West region a half-hour, black and white documentary about the Warminster mystery titled *Pie in the Sky*. Despite the inauspicious broadcast date, the documentary was level-headed and fair, although the presenter did, at times, seem to be more than amused by what local people told him. These locals, however, appear to be sincere, and genuinely puzzled by the events they are describing. The general conclusion of the documentary was that reports of the Thing were most likely a result of military activity on the Plain, perhaps tests of then state-of-the-art technology.

Whatever the conclusions of the documentary, the BBC had once again provided legitimacy to the Warminster mystery, and had again provided, to those curious about UFOs, information about a location of interest should they choose to travel to it. Such people *were* choosing to travel to Warminster, and while there, often met the man who had become the nexus about which all mystery whirled – Arthur Shuttlewood.

The A-Team

It is unknown when Arthur Shuttlewood assembled his own "investigative" skywatching team, but there are many reports in the books Shuttlewood was to later write of sightings by his "team". The team included himself, Bob Strong, an ex-RAF war-time bomber-crew member, and Sybil Champion.

Bob Strong was the photographer for the team and, over the next few years, amassed a large library of images of the objects seen in the night-time skies around the town. Shuttlewood noted that, from February 1966 to March 1968, Bob Strong took 3,523 photos "of which only 101 have developed convincingly". Shuttlewood nonetheless claimed that these photographs comprised the "finest collection of authentic pictures in the world, of their specialist kind". (*Warnings From Flying Friends*, p.41)

Bob Strong's photographs – and Arthur Shuttlewood's claims – have to be viewed with a certain amount of scepticism. If the photographs in Shuttlewood's books are a sample of the 101 that "developed convincingly", we cannot imagine how bad the other 3422 were. The photographs taken by Bob Strong that Shuttlewood selected for inclusion in his books are unclear, indistinct, blurred, or possibly, hoaxes. Certainly, there is nothing in Bob Strong's collection of photographs as immediately impressive as the Faulkner photograph.

For example, the following photograph is reproduced in Shuttlewood's *Warnings From Flying Friends,* where it is captioned *February 28th, 1966. Angled shot of disc at night by Bob Strong, from Cradle Hill*. If this is not an intentional fake, it is almost certainly a processing fault. How do we know? Kevin Goodman was a keen amateur photographer during the 1970s, and developed his own black and white film. He knows how easy it is to unintentionally pinch a roll of negative film during the development process. This picture is a classic case of a negative pinch, similar to ones Kevin had himself accidentally created.

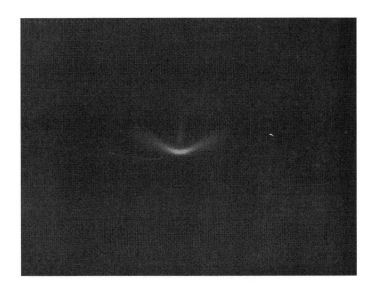

With Shuttlewood – following his own sighting in September the previous year – now a convinced believer that the Thing represented examples of extraterrestrial craft, and a skywatcher with his own "investigative" skywatching team, UFO sightings from him and his team also began to feed into the Warminster mystery. These sightings were then to make their way into Shuttlewood's books.

Shuttlewood Writes a Book

Just before the *Warminster Journal* stopped printing stories about the Thing, towards the tail-end of 1965, Shuttlewood had written a short article in which he requested any readers who had not yet contacted him with UFO reports to do so, as he intended writing a book about the mystery. Shuttlewood had, by now, amassed a sizeable file of reports of UFO sightings and mysterious noises. Writing a book about the Warminster mystery was an obvious step to take for a seasoned journalist.

That he already had a publisher is evidenced by Brinsley Le Poer Trench's book, *The Flying Saucer Story*, published by Neville Spearman in 1966, which contains a short advertisement for a forthcoming book, *The Warminster Sighting* by Arthur Shuttlewood. The advertisement promises that the book will contain details of Faulkner's photograph, and "the many subsequent contacts experienced by the author in the Warminster area". It was to be another year before the book was published, in May 1967, during which time many more reports were to reach Shuttlewood, and many other interesting things were to occur, all of which would help Shuttlewood fill the pages of the book.

Warminster Week

If it took the occasional media event to spark sighting reports from previously sceptical Warminster residents, no such impetus was required to convince the skywatchers, ufologists and ufological societies that something big, important and ufological was happening in and around the town. Something so big, and so important, needed a big and important research effort. To this end, the British UFO Research Association (BUFORA) organised Warminster Week, a research effort directed by John Cleary-Baker. Warminster Week took place over the last week of July, 1966 (23rd-30th) – a week, Ken Rogers remembers, of rain, cloud and unseasonably cold nights.

SKY WATCH OVER WARMINTSER

IF any space travellers decide to land in or around Warminster next week there will be a reception committee waiting for them.

From tomorrow, members of the British UFO Research Association —the people who firmly believe in "things from space"—will be keeping a round-the-clock watch on the Warminster sky.

And there on Wednesday night to try and make contact with the travellers will be Dr. John Cleary-Baker, chief evaluating officer for BUFORA, who is supervising the week's operation.

Warminster Week is described in detail in *The Warminster Triangle.* (pp.41-43) The research effort involved three observation posts manned by volunteers from BUFORA, who would observe the night skies and log any UFOs observed. The posts were established at Warminster's Cradle Hill and Cley Hill, and at White Horse Hill on the downs above Westbury. The White Horse Hill observation post was, however, "abandoned after two days, owing to communication difficulties and a total lack of results". Warminster Week was hampered, according to Rogers, not only by the weather, but by an "invasion of journalists, camera crews, TV interviewers, and the like, intrigued by the project, the first of its kind to be launched".

The results of Warminster Week were not very impressive. A few lights in the sky, some easily identified satellites, and a lot of army flak. That the army were so active that week suggests that some of the reported unidentified lights in the sky could simply have been military ordnance outside the experience of the observers.

Touring the Area

Meanwhile, the residents of Warminster and the local villages continued to report sightings of the Thing to Shuttlewood. In June 1966, Mrs Marson reported a "loud humming in the night, with thumping sounds", and later saw "a brilliant white light which lit up our bedroom bright as day". (*The Warminster Mystery*, p.21)

Dennis Tilt and his wife were driving back to Warminster across Salisbury Plain on the night of October 22nd, when they spotted the Thing. First encountering it as three flame-coloured lights in a field by the road, Mr Tilt stopped the car and warily investigated, until his nervous wife encouraged him to return to the car and carry on back to Warminster. Mr Tilt did so, but the lights appeared to rise into the sky and follow them back to Warminster, only fading from their sight when they reached their home. The couple were so sure they had seen something unusual that Mr Tilt returned to investigate the field the next day, and talked to the farmer.

The Thing appeared also to be expanding its area of operations somewhat, with sightings late in the year in Westbury, Trowbridge and Chippenham. Despite having spread its wings, the Thing˙ remained mainly associated with Warminster and its environs. Even though the number of UFO sightings had appeared to fall away slightly February, 1966 had continued be active. What would 1967 bring?

Still Flapping – 1967-1968

In 1967, Arthur Shuttlewood's first book was published. *The Warminster Sighting* had obviously been a working title; when the book was finally published by Neville Spearman, the title had changed to the more familiar and possibly punchier *The Warminster Mystery*, a title which over time was to provide the epithet that encompassed everything that constituted the phenomena occurring around the town – lights in the sky, noises, mysterious men, invisible walkers and so on – and had now come to be associated with the Thing itself.

The Warminster Mystery

The Warminster Mystery is an interesting book, if one can cope with Shuttlewood's rather flowery prose, and is also perhaps one of the more important books in UFO history. It is not only us who believe this; in *Cults of Unreason*, Christopher Evans calls *The Warminster Mystery* "a minor classic of its kind". It is important because it describes the genesis of the phenomenon, the conversion of a 'disbeliever', the increasing 'devotion' of Shuttlewood to revealing 'the truth', and the increasingly *avant-garde* theories and hypotheses put forward to explain the phenomenon. In this and the rest of Shuttlewood's books we are presented with the gallimaufry –

obsessives, mystics, and other sideshows – of the UFO phenomena.

The Warminster Mystery provided detailed information on the reports that Shuttlewood had received about the Thing. It also included Shuttlewood's own thoughts on the nature of the phenomena, as well the theories, hypotheses and notions of people who had been corresponding with Shuttlewood. One element of Shuttlewood's thinking that might have surprised some readers was the religious nature of it.

That Shuttlewood used a rather dense, flowery prose style is perhaps one of the reasons why the book had the impact that it did, and helped to define the nature of the Warminster mystery. Dewey and Ries, in *In Alien Heat*, provide an analysis of the language used in Shuttlewood's book. We will only note here that for those reports described in both the *Warminster Journal* and *The Warminster Mystery*, it is obvious how much more dramatic Shuttlewood made events when he described them in *The Warminster Mystery*. Without access to Shuttlewood's notebooks, it is, of course, impossible to know which of the narrative styles most accurately reflects the descriptions of sightings reported to Shuttlewood. Nonetheless, for those readers not yet aware of the nature of most Warminster UFO sightings (which were, commonly, simply lights in the sky), the dramatic language of *The Warminster Mystery* must have helped them believe that something mysterious and exciting was occurring in and around Warminster.

It was in *The Warminster Mystery* that the contacts with the Aenstrians, which occurred in September and October 1965, are first described for an audience outside of Shuttlewood's circle of acquaintances (see the previous chapter for a discussion of these contacts). The description of these contacts can only have added a further layer of intrigue to the mystery and, again, might well have excited readers enough to want to visit hills around the town.

The Whole Country Flaps

In 1967, there were UFO flaps across the entire country. UFOs were seen in, for example, Hampshire and Devon, as well as Warminster. October 1967 was a particularly busy month. As Ian Ridpath notes, "a rash of UFO sightings occurred over Britain. Many of these made it no further than the pages of the press, but some were reported to the Ministry of Defence".* We wonder if the speculation that surrounded the Warminster mystery, which had been popularised by Shuttlewood in the national press over the preceding two years, had encouraged people to look for mysteries in the skies.

Possibly the most famous of the 1967 cases is that of the *Devon flying cross*. This sighting was reported in national newspapers, and on television news. The event involved two policemen in a police car who, while on patrol, sighted the UFO near Okehampton in the early hours of the morning of 24th October. They chased the UFO for over thirty miles at speeds of up to 80 or 90 miles per hour, before the UFO eventually disappeared at about five o'clock in the morning. That the witnesses to the UFO were policemen no doubt added verisimilitude to the sighting, and the reports of their car

---

* **http://www.ianridpath.com/ufo/octoberflap.htm**, accessed 16/04/2011.

chase along the quiet Devon roads would have increased the drama.

Nobody could have predicted such a sighting except, perhaps, Arthur Shuttlewood himself; he had gained inside information on future dramatic UFO events from an unexpected source.

Shuttlewood Meets Karne

Shuttlewood had, it turned out, indeed predicted such sightings to various people, including Dr John Cleary-Baker of BUFORA. Soon after the Devon UFO sighting described above, Shuttlewood received a letter from Cleary-Baker in which he called Shuttlewood "a downy old bird" and added "how on Earth did you know?" (*Warnings From Flying Friends*, pp.94-95) Shuttlewood knew because he had been visited, on May 28th, 1967, by another Aenstrian. On that day, Karne the Aenstrian phoned Shuttlewood to express his disappointment that *The Warminster Mystery* had implied the Aenstrian contacts might have been hoaxes. Shuttlewood, grumpy from too much work and too much skywatching, argued that as a journalist he took nothing on faith, and that telephone calls from Aenstrians strained his credulity. Karne argued that there had to be mutual trust; if Shuttlewood continued to doubt the existence and validity of his contacts, then all contact would stop, and the messages the Aenstrians had for the world would go unheard. Shuttlewood told Karne that as a journalist, he would have more faith in his interlocutors if they talked to him in the flesh. That, it appears, was all the persuasion Karne needed. Within seven seconds, Karne was knocking at Shuttlewood's front door. (*Warnings*

From Flying Friends, p.198.) In passing, one can't help but wonder why Karne preferred as his medium a journalist on a parochial newspaper rather than, say journalists at the BBC or ITV.

Having lambasted Shuttlewood for not believing in the reality of the Aenstrians, Karne generously gave Shuttlewood nine minutes of his time. During those nine minutes, Karne warned Shuttlewood that "Earth time is desperately short", and then voiced various dire warnings: the magnetic balance of Earth had been disturbed by changes around the "inner core"; the death of civilisation and its replacement by a "new and glorious age" would occur; those who were prepared – who believed in UFOs and the Second Coming of Christ – "would have much work to do in necessary recon-struction". The conversation seemed to wander around these topics for the short time Karne had allotted for this interview. Shuttlewood asked if Karne knew when predictions would come to pass, but, of course, Karne did not. (*Warnings From Flying Friends*, p.199-209.) It was during this conversation that Karne mentioned that other objects and lights would be seen, among which would be flying crosses.

Shuttlewood duly reported this visit by Karne in a chapter in *Warnings From Flying Friends*, published in 1968. It is obvious from the tenor of this chapter that, after meeting Karne, Shuttlewood was now ready to believe that Aenstrians were real, were alien, and that their messages were genuine. Having demonstrated his belief in the Aenstrians by describing Karne's visit in his next book, Shuttlewood is never visited or contacted by them again. Moral? Never trust an Aenstrian.

Sightings Continue

UFO sightings around Warminster continued through 1967 and 1968, even though there was no longer the buzz and excitement associated with the early days of the mystery. Perhaps sensing that the excitement was fading, Shuttlewood wrote:

'Are UFOs still appearing over Warminster?' In answer to hosts of inquiring letters I have received ... the short and honest reply is: 'Yes'. (*Warnings From Flying Friends*, p.14)

Yet there is a sense now that the UFO phenomenon in Warminster had become *mundane*. After the early years – when the mystery had been the subject of television programmes and newspaper articles, and there had been journalists in the area, meetings at the town hall, and all the rest of the hoopla – things had settled down. UFO sightings had become common, almost routine. The number of sightings reported had fallen somewhat in comparison to the early days. Yet the phenomenon continued. The Thing continued to flit about the Warminster skies, Shuttlewood diligently recorded sightings of it, and went to Cradle Hill to skywatch with his own small team.

Even if the existence of the mystery was now mundane, still there was a place for events that were quite extraordinary. An unusual UFO sighting and contact was reported to Shuttlewood in January 1968. After previously seeing a UFO, a man received a telephone call urging him to go to Heaven's Gate, a popular beauty spot, at a particular time and date. The man, accompanied by a woman, duly kept the appointment. Three minutes past the appointed hour, the woman saw a UFO flying in front of Heaven's Gate. The UFO dropped down to the ground. The man and woman ran towards the object. When they arrived at the place it had landed, they found the UFO to be barely bigger than a soup-plate. A tiny, golden ladder appeared beneath the UFO and about two dozen, 4-inch high figures climbed down. Stepping away from the object, each figure grew to normal human size in front of the rather dumbstruck man and woman. The aliens shook hands with them, and the engaged in pleasantries. After a few minutes the aliens invited the man on a trip with them in their UFO to see some of the "hidden wonders of his world." The man, no longer fearful, agreed. He left his car keys and effects with the woman, and then he shrank, along with the rest of the aliens. They all boarded the tiny spaceship which then, with a whistling sound, took off and soared away. The woman waited on the hill for another eight hours, before the man returned. (This sighting is des-cribed in *The Warminster Triangle*, p. 92.)

Shuttlewood continued to hear, from fellow sky-watchers and correspondents, theories and ideas about the nature of the Thing, and about the paranormal phenomena that now seemed inseparable from it. There was so much to relate, and no outlet. Time then, for a new book.

Warnings From Flying Friends

Shuttlewood reported the UFO sightings that had occurred from mid-1966 through to 1968 in his next book, *Warnings From Flying Friends*. Despite the excite-ment generated by the Thing, sales ot *The Warminster Mystery* had done little to encourage Shuttlewood's pub-lishers, Neville Spearman, to commission a second book.

Shuttlewood's *Warnings From Flying Friends* was self-published in 1968 (indeed, copies could still be purchased in 1977, as advertisements in the local UFO magazines testify). *Warnings From Flying Friends* contains not only reports of UFO sightings, but theoretical, speculative ideas about UFOs and the UFO subject. Sometimes these ideas appear to be Shuttlewood's own; while some chapters and long sections of chapters are devoted to correspondents whose names root them in Christian theology – Mark and Thomas. There is the meeting with Karne the Aenstrian, referred to in the section above. Mixed into this hodgepodge are the descriptions of UFO sightings.

The Warminster Mystery had the marketing back-up of a large publishing house, and would have been available in book-shops to the casual browser, feeding the curiosity of those interested in UFOs. As *Warnings From Flying Friends* was self-published, however, there were few marketing channels for the book, and few distribution outlets. The only places Shuttlewood could have advertised – or at least made ufologists aware of the book's existence – would have been the ufological magazines, and at the lectures Shuttlewood sometimes gave at conferences. The ufological magazines were small-scale ventures, and the conference circuit less well-developed than it now is. The continuing availability of *Warnings from Flying Friends* in the 1977, in the days before print-on-demand, indicates that the book was to be a slow seller. It could thus never reach the audience *The Warminster Mystery* did; it could never, therefore, have encouraged the curious to visit Warminster in the same numbers they once had.

Even if *Warnings From Flying Friends* had found a mainstream publisher, it is unlikely that it would have touched as many people as *The Warminster Mystery*; it is, in comparison, a more difficult, a more esoteric, book. *The Warminster Mystery* was exciting – it reported extraordinary events that had occurred around and above a small town in Great Britain, rather than the United States, the usual locus of such tales. The Thing had exploded onto the scene with sonic assaults, dazzling orbs and speeding spheres, and the language of *The Warminster Mystery* reflected that. *Warnings from Flying Friends* couldn't maintain that excitement; by the time it was published, the phenomena around the town had been occurring (and had remained mysterious) for three years. The mystery had become routine, mundane. Of course there were still UFO sightings – this was, after all, Warminster, where reports of unusual lights and sounds numbered over a thousand by this time. Yet these are not the focus of *Warnings from Flying Friends*. The book focuses instead mainly on possible explanations for the phenomena, ideas about the nature of it and on Shuttlewood's correspondents: the epiphenomena surrounding the phenomenon. It is these, as much as the Thing itself, that were creating the context out of which the content was being crafted.

The Continuing Mystery

Throughout 1969, the silver spheroids continued to sail sedately and serenely across the starry skies above Warminster; amber gambollers still ambled and gambolled for curious skywatchers. The phenomenon now had a momentum of its own; the media was no longer important. UFOs continued to be reported; the curious still came to Warminster; casual visitors became regular skywatchers who visited each weekend and positioned themselves on the slopes and summits of Cradle Hill and Cley Hill, waiting and watching. If the number of people visiting the hills no longer reached the scale witnessed in 1965-1967, still the "earnest seekers after truth", as Shuttlewood called them, headed to Warminster, hoping for a sighting, a landing, contact, mystery, wonder and awe.

For years, Shuttlewood had been the central contact point for skywatchers and journalists. There was no Warminster UFO Research Group, no Warminster Aerial Phenomena Group, no Warminster Anomalous Sky Phenomena Research and Investigation Organisation. The other research groups visited – BUFORA, *FSR*, MUFORG, KUFORG and others in the alphabetty-spaghetti of British ufology – but in Warminster, Shuttlewood and his loyal skywatching team dominated the discourse.

This was to change, however, during the 1970s.

Things Begin to Change 1970-1974

At the beginning of 1970, UFOs had been haunting Warminster for just over five years. Arthur Shuttlewood had made the town famous – at least to those interested in UFOs and aliens – world-wide. The town went about its quotidian business, ignoring the influx of hippies, mystics and other followers of the New Age. Local businesses were probably happy with Shuttlewood's efforts to proselytise the mystery, as it boosted tourism. There were, of course, still UFOs to be seen. The first UFO sighting that Shuttlewood describes, in *UFOs - Key to the New Age*, the book he published in 1970, is from the 18th of January of that year.

The Excitement Continues

On a damp night at Cradle Hill, Shuttlewood sat with John Roseweir, the former national vice-chairman of Contact UK, in Roseweir's car. They saw something most:

> singular because it produced the first UFO of this extraordinary type ever seen in our portion of the world and scattered further threads from cosmic cobwebs of complexity. (*UFOs–Key to the New Age*, pp.90-91)

As ever, the UFO "silently ... glided into view" and then hovered for a total of twenty seconds. Shuttlewood described an ellipsoid that was:

> pure gold in colour and suspended at a height of about fifty feet above ground level, between the wooded eminence of Cop Heap and the sloping shoulder of the Warminster downs...

> Over the sun-disc aero-form was a silvery plume ... motionless and unwavering ... From the bottom half of the UFO a dark triangle or pyramid shape was clearly visible at a later phase before blackout. We both estimated the craft to be no more than a mile distant ... the ellipsoid probably of thirty feet overall dimension as it met our wondering gaze...

Shuttlewood and Roseweir had, before their sighting, been discussing:

> Megalithic crosses and monoliths, also the recurrence of the figures "3" and "9" in progressive stages of UFO sightings and research... Now, on January 18th, 1970 (1+8=9) at 9.30pm (another "9" and "3"), the dark pyramid appendage dangling from the lower outline of the UFO seemed to sidle sideways and land at a sector near the slopes of Cop Heap after the glowing golden craft winked brightly three times and vanished.

Shuttlewood pontificates:

> The unmoving silver flame that vied with the gold, the plume at the top dissolved simultaneously. What did it all mean? And how often have we wondered precisely that, after numerous strange sightings on Cradle Hill!

We see, then, that the sightings still generate excitement for Shuttlewood; they still glide into view, they are still lambent and golden. They still, by their very presence and their mode of display, present questions – questions that were to shape and define Shuttlewood's third book, *UFOs - Key to the New Age*. They were questions that would give rise to more questions; questions that would go unanswered – because, after all, the Warminster mystery still remains a mystery.

Hoaxing Things

Hoaxing has always been a confounding problem at Warminster. Although UFO sightings and reports are sometimes dismissed as hoaxes, and hoaxes are discussed in particular terms when they are identified, hoaxing itself is a phenomenon about which we hear very little. Hoaxers themselves rarely discuss their work – after all, the power of a hoax diminishes if the truth about it is revealed. At the same time, believers in UFO reality do not want to contemplate the magnitude of the problem (as the more recent and continuing debate over hoaxed crop circles testifies).

The Society for the Investigation of UFO Phenomenon (SIUFOP) began perpetrating hoaxes at Warminster in the late 1960s. SIUFOP was formed in the 1960s by a group of young friends interested in the UFO phenomenon. As David Simpson, a SIUFOP member at the time, writes:

> Several in the group were, or were training to be scientists of one form or another and felt in a good position to bring some technical skills to bear in analysing the reports. (*Conclusions from Controlled UFO Hoaxes*, p.5)

SIUFOP conducted skywatches from local hills and interviewed UFO witnesses. They were initially excited by a phenomenon they at first believed to be evidence of something exotic and out of the ordinary. The beliefs of the group members quickly changed, however. A UFO they had seen – a sighting that had thrilled them at the time – was, they realised after analysis, simply car headlights on a distant hill. Simpson writes: "it is difficult to believe that tiredness and enthusiasm could have warped our observational skills so much". (Ibid., p.7) Reports of UFOs they heard while skywatching on the South Downs were, they noted, transmuting with subsequent retellings. Nonetheless, still having a reserve of enthusiasm, they assumed that UFO sightings elsewhere "would be more robust".

The search for these more robust UFO sightings led them to Warminster. SIUFOP members were shown photographs that were claimed to be good evidence of UFO sightings. SIUFOP invariably found that the photographs could be replicated by photographing mundane sky phenomena, such as satellites and space debris, or by photographing the lights on domestic appliances. They had also seen, as we subsequently did, the excitement engendered by typical stimuli seen from the hills, such as satellites, flares, or stars. Scepticism was setting in.

When discussing their scepticism with skywatchers, SIUFOP were met with derision. They simply had to believe; they were not open-minded enough; they were too critical in their evaluations. They were also told that their "results and methods amounted to calling UFO witnesses fools and liars and did the subject a lot of harm". (Ibid., p.5) Such unscientific attitudes did little to dissaude SIUFOP. Being scientists (or scientists manqué) they decided to undertake some new experiments that would enable them to objectively assess the observational and investigative abilities of ufologists. To do this, they would have to know the qualities of the stimuli presented to skywatchers and ufologists. Thus they were led to begin hoaxing UFOs.

SIUFOP began their experiments on the hills in Sussex, but soon moved their experiments to Warminster. They continued their experiments over subsequent years, even using kites to lift lights with delayed timers. SIUFOP found in their early experiments that there were often confounding co-variables that they couldn't control. For example, one night they hoaxed a UFO, but then a UFO reportedly similar to their hoax had been seen on the subsequent night. Attempting to convince skywatchers that the UFO on the first night *had* been their hoax, and that the UFO seen the next night *had not* been a hoax, led to accusations that the hoaxers were hoaxing (that is, lying about their hoax – indicating what a tangled web hoaxing becomes) in an attempt to distract skywatchers from Warminster's mystery. What SIUFOP needed was a UFO that could be more tightly controlled. Enter the appropriately named Mr. Foxwell.

SIUFOP placed a brilliant light on top of a car. In front of the light was placed a purple filter. The light was switched on for five seconds, off for five seconds, and then on again for 25 seconds. A hoax UFO detector placed at Cradle Hill by SIUFOP sounded about fifteen seconds after the light was illuminated. UFO detectors were supposedly able to detect changes in terrestrial magnetic fields caused by passing UFOs. Skywatchers at Warminster observed the light, and their general belief was that they had seen a UFO. One of the witnesses was a Norman Foxwell, who took two photographs of the UFO. Foxwell's part in the hoax was to pass on the film to be developed by any enthusiastic UFO researcher present on the hill that night. He passed the negatives to John Ben, who had contacts within *Flying Saucer Review*, and had also been a witness to the events that night. Two of the photographs on the film had, in fact, been taken by SIUFOP previous to that night. Foxwell had only taken a further two photographs, of the nightscape after the light had been turned off. The hoaxed exposures showed a UFO that looked nothing like the light that had been illuminated that night.

John Ben developed the photographs and reported the sighting in Issue No 4, Volume 16, of the *Flying Saucer Review*. That the sightings and photographs were a hoax was leaked in 1972, at which point *FSR* published a full retraction.

The hoax highlights how what witnesses thought they had observed differed from the actual stimulus, and also how a ufological investigation was subsequently handled. The description of the "UFO" provided by John Ben in his article in *Flying Saucer Review* more closely matches the photographs than the actual stimulus provided by the object at Warminster. SIUFOP pointed out that there were many clues in the pictures that should have indicated that they were fakes, and that no-one from *FSR* had ever interviewed the photographer, Norman Foxwell. The hoax is important in that it demonstrates how easily simple lights in the sky can be misinterpreted, and how easily photographic evidence can be hoaxed and dupe investigators.

In 1972, SIUFOP spoofed a skywatch at which the BBC was participating. Ufologists interviewed by the BBC claimed that SIUFOP's hoaxes were the best UFOs they had ever seen. After the story broke on BBC's *Nationwide*

FLYING
SAUCER
REVIEW

fsr

Vol. 16, No. 4   July/August 1970   Five Shillings

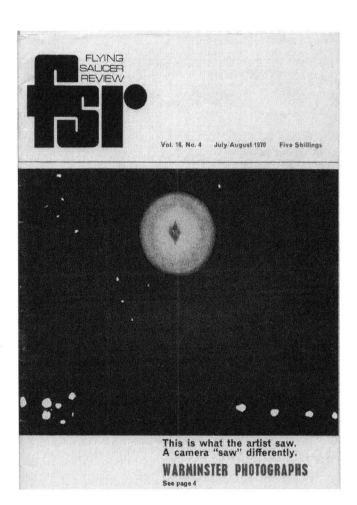

This is what the artist saw.
A camera "saw" differently.

WARMINSTER PHOTOGRAPHS

See page 4

programme, the SIUFOP members admitted to their involvement. They were subsequently interviewed on *Nationwide*, along with the ufologist Rex Dutta, who refused to believe that he had been hoaxed. The BBC asked for a re-enactment, at which Dutta was present. The weather was less favourable, and when Dutta saw the lights, he said they were unlike the lights previously seen, and obviously lights on a balloon. Given that he now knew the actual source of the lights, his conclusion seems inevitable. (David Simpson and Ken Raine, 'An Account of Experimental UFO Hoaxing', *Magonia*, July 2001, pp.13-16.)

Was Arthur Shuttlewood aware of the hoaxes and the hoaxers? The testimony of Molly Carey, recounted on David Simpson's DVD, *Warminster, Cradle Hill and UFOs: Some Recollections by Molly Carey*, indicates that Shuttlewood might have been. Molly feels that Shuttlewood must have known that some of the objects seen at skywatches were hoaxes. However, because Shuttlewood "never wanted people to come without seeing something", he didn't contradict those who believed they saw Things that were possibly a torch attached to a kite. The astute Molly also recognises that the witnesses wanted to believe that the Things they were seeing were something mysterious, something more than a torch.

The 1972 hoax described above was, David Simpson asserts in *Conclusions from Controlled UFO Hoaxes*, the final hoax.* Reading David Simpson's account of his experiments causes us to wonder how many other

---

* Note that both current authors have met David Simpson many times, and are on cordial terms with the mountebank.

groups and individuals carried out informal 'experiments' around Warminster.

UFOs - Key to the New Age

UFOs - Key to the New Age, published in 1971, is – of all the six books that Shuttlewood wrote about the Warminster mystery over the course of twelve years – by far the most outlandish. More than ever, Shuttlewood takes the opportunity to voice his own ideas about the UFOs and their occupants – how the craft are propelled, the mission of the aliens here on Earth, how UFOs connect to other religions, teachings, and mysticisms. Everything connects. If T. S. Eliot, in *The Waste Land*, can connect nothing with nothing, the New Age grabs threads and reconnects promiscuously – everything connects, with everything.

Shuttlewood attempts to enter the web and find the connections between everything he has seen, heard and learned – the ideas that have been raised in *The Warminster Mystery* and, particularly, in *Warnings From Flying Friends* – and his beloved UFOs. Take for example, his claims that the numbers 3 and 9, alluded to in the UFO sighting above, have some special significance. During skywatches, he and others would often flash their powerful torches at any UFO they saw in a pattern consisting of three flashes, then a short gap, another three flashes, another gap, and then a final three flashes. Shuttlewood claimed that the objects responded to these signals, often changing course or flashing back. Shuttlewood devotes seven or eight pages of a chapter entitled 'Great Truths Forming in the Void' in *UFOs -*

Key to the New Age to the numbers three and nine, and to pyramids. Everything connects.

Shuttlewood also devotes chapters to 'Investigating the Fourth Dimension', 'Gravity and Terrestrial Substances', 'Big Bang, Steady State, or Pulsation', and 'Great Truths Forming in the Void'. Everything connects. Dewey and Ries, in *In Alien Heat*, analyse *UFOs - Key to the New Age* in depth; interested readers should refer to that book for more information.

What is obvious, even to the most devoted follower of Warminster's mystery, is that there are fewer UFO sighting reports in *UFOs - Key to the New Age* than in previous books. One can speculate why this should be: perhaps there are fewer UFO sightings to report; alternatively, perhaps even Shuttlewood realised that endless lists of lights-in-the-sky can be tedious, and preferred to use the medium of his new book mainly for speculation.

One Pair of Eyes

In May 1970, the BBC transmitted a somewhat light-hearted documentary, presented by Patrick Moore, about independent thinkers and obscure belief systems. Entitled *One Pair of Eyes,* the programme described a wide range of beliefs, including a man who believed the Earth to be flat, and the Aetherius Society, the quasi-religious movement founded by ex-London taxi driver George King., who had been contacted by aliens in 1954.

On December 31st 1969, Patrick Moore and a BBC crew travelled to Cradle Hill to film Arthur Shuttlewood for the programme. Shuttlewood later claimed that the programme had been severely edited before transmission, thus diminishing the impact of certain events that occurred that night. As Shuttlewood writes:

> Although [the film crew] were at Warminster twenty-four hours, spending several hours in filming and interviewing, only about five minutes of carefully edited film found its way into the actual programme.

What particularly irked Shuttlewood was that he believed something unusual had been seen and filmed on the night of the skywatch and that this had been glossed over. He wrote:

> People must have been left wondering, because the fact was obscured: Did Patrick Moore see anything unidentifiable or not? For there were precious few clues in the disjointed programme to indicate yea or nay.

The answer, as far as Shuttlewood was concerned, was a resounding *yes*; Moore *had* seen something unusual:

> You can accept my solemn word for it that he did – and his unusual visual experience was shared by the whole thrilled unit [...] at two minutes to 9.00pm beneath a perfectly cloudless sky [...] an orange glow ... developed into the shape of an ellipsoid craft flying low...

The sighting began to take on even more characteristics of a Warminster UFO:

> It hovered briefly over the tree line, no farther from the eye than 500 yards, and fewer than thirty five feet in altitude when hovering. It had a typical duck-bobbing forward motion, elegant and effortless in flight. It abruptly disappeared after a sixty second display of aerial magic. Then, as noiseless and as graceful as the first, another flying shape caught all fascinated eyes as it "broke" from a similar part of the sky. It was slightly smaller in dimension, although bearing identical contours and colouring. It came into view almost a minute after its predecessor, dipping low near the tree line and floating below the copse at nearest point, at the far side, a

> beautiful ribbon of rainbow light tracing its path...
> (*UFOs–Key to the New Age*, pp.11-14)

Shuttlewood said that Moore and his colleagues were quietly thrilled by the mystical quality of the "near landings of soundless wonders that have so frequently haunted Cradle Hill for six years". Moore said that they were a mystery – not what he would call unidentified flying objects, but "simply fascinating and inexplicable light formations".

If you read Moore's account of the sighting, and watch the documentary, it is easy to see where the disagreements lie. In both the book *Can You Speak Venusian?* and the documentary *One Pair of Eyes*, it is patently obvious that Moore was not convinced that what he and the crew had observed was, in fact, a 'genuine' UFO. As Moore says in his book:

> there was a difference of opinion; Arthur maintained it was connected with the interplanetary craft, and rejected my suggestion that it was a low lying cloud illuminated by the Moon. (Patrick Moore, *Can you speak Venusian?*, p.106-107)

Dewey and Ries discuss this particular episode from Warminster's colourful UFO history in *In Alien Heat*.

Whichever account of what occurred is the most accurate, Shuttlewood felt the programme belittled and discredited him and his fellow researchers. From that day, he refused to have any more dealings with the BBC – until, at least, 1977.

The Warminster UFO Newsletter

As we noted at the end of the previous chapter, there were no UFO groups in Warminster similar to BUFORA or MUFORG – instead, there was Shuttlewood, who had, for a long time, been the single, single-minded champion of the Warminster mystery. As the Warminster mystery moved into the 1970s, however, the situation was to slowly change. A subtle sign of this change was the publication of the first local magazine (or fanzine, even) that addressed the Warminster UFO phenomenon. That it took so long for a local UFO magazine to be produced is a surprise; that it was *not* produced by Shuttlewood – with his journalistic experience and connections, through the *Warminster Journal*, with Coates and Parker the local printers – is another surprise.

Ken Rogers had been, for some time, a semi-regular visitor to the hills around the town; he had an interest an in UFOs, and was a member of the International Sky Scouts. What Rogers had heard about the events in Warminster had so intrigued him he had moved from London and settled in the town so that that he could better study both ufology and the Warminster mystery. Rogers struck up a friendship with Arthur Shuttlewood and spent many hours on the local hills as a member of Arthur Shuttlewood's observing team.

It was to be Ken Rogers, then, who published Warminster's first UFO magazine. The first edition of the *Warminster UFO Newsletter* is dated August, 1971. Ken Rogers edited the magazine, and undoubtedly wrote some of the articles; he probably also published it, on a hand-cranked mimeograph.

The intention of the magazine was to document the sightings and events in the Warminster area. It also, in best New Age fashion, attempted to connect everything with everything; later issues thus also described the local

Warminster Newsletter

No. 10   OCTOBER 1972   10p.

folklore and forteana. The *Newsletter* was to be the template for the Warminster-based magazines that were to follow it in the 1970s. Rogers was assisted by Arthur Shuttlewood and John Cleary-Baker, editor of BUFORA's *Journal*, both of whom penned articles for the *Newsletter*. Cleary-Baker's involvement is a sign of his obvious fascination with the Warminster mystery, having also been a contributor to the letters page of *The Warminster Journal*, where he had defended the Thing from its detractors.

The first issue of the magazine was a pilot, to gauge interest in the venture. Rogers began publishing the *Newsletter* monthly from January 1972, with a cover price of 10p. A year's subscription, costing £1.10, offered a saving of 10p. From issue 5 onwards – perhaps because of the dearth of local sightings – Rogers began a feature on local myths and legends, some of which were to make more than one appearance in the pages of the *Newsletter*. Relevant press cuttings from further afield appeared frequently, as did a regular column – 'One World, One Truth' – that contained excerpts from a book written by Johan Quanjar (who was also an International Sky Scout).

The last issue of the *Newsletter* that we know of is that of March/April 1973 (Number 14/15). We do not know if there were any further issues. If 14/15 *is* the last issue, it is interesting to note that the *Newsletter* seems to have faded away just after a revamp of its editorial board and a redesign of its pages. 14/15 also seemed to be the most fact-packed issue – the *Newsletter* appeared to be on the up. (Facsimiles of the *Warminster UFO Newsletter* can be found at *UFO Warminster* (**www.ufo-warminster.co.uk**).

The Warminster Mystery is Republished

Somewhere around 1972, between the ages of 13 and 14, one of the current authors [Steve] began to frequent the local hills with his friends. We made silver death masks out of tin-foil in the golf course bunkers at night, we frightened ourselves in graveyards at dusk, and we walked to Cradle Hill copse in the dark and spooked each other out. We bought the *Warminster UFO Newsletter*, and began to read books about the occult. Then in 1973, *The Warminster Mystery* was re-released in paperback by Tandem Books. We finally realised just how excitingly weird was the town in which we lived.

Despite the paucity of UFO reports in the *Warminster UFO Newsletter*, there was at least a long list in Issue 2 of the UFO sightings that been reported in 1971. The list showed that at least one UFO had been reported each month. Sightings continued throughout the life of the *Newsletter*, yet at nowhere near the frequency of the late 1960s. If there had been a graph of UFO sightings over time, the slope of the line would have been decidedly downward.

Yet the dogged faithful returned again and again to the hills around the town, and in particular to Cradle Hill. And with the republication of *The Warminster Mystery*, now backed by the marketing power of a mainstream publisher like Tandem, a new audience was to discover and rediscover the mystery. During the early to mid-70s, there was an interesting resurgence in UFO book publishing, with Tandem and Sphere leading the way. Jacques Vallee, Ivan T. Sanderson, Donald Keyhoe, Brinsley Le Poer Trench and Brad Steiger were among the ufological and fortean luminaries to have their books published or republished in paperback during this period. Because of this flood of cheap and accessible UFO material, Kevin – the other author of this book – was overwhelmed with information about UFOs – a subject in which he'd only recently become interested – and finally discovered that there was a place in the UK as exciting as anything he'd read about in the Americas. That place was, of course, Warminster.

From the early 1970s through to at least 1976, during spring and summer weekends, Cradle Hill would be visited by eager groups of skywatchers; sometimes twenty or thirty, sometimes even more. One can only speculate what effect cheap, mass market paperbacks had on increasing the numbers that took to skywatching on Warminster's hills, and what those new, eager, excited skywatchers thought they were seeing. We know that these books affected at least some skywatchers – Kevin and *his* friends, and Steve and *his* friends; we can at least assume then that the same holds for others who became ufologists and skywatchers.

The Quiet Year

The excitements of the previous few years had now calmed. That UFOs were still seen is not doubted; there were ample skywatchers who had been encouraged to return again and again by *something*. Yet 1974 saw no new books by Shuttlewood; the *Warminster UFO Newsletter* seems to have folded and no new magazines rose to take its place. Outwardly, 1974 was probably the quietest year in the nine-year life of the Warminster mystery. Warminster had, by this time, been subject to critical appraisals from such organisations as the Merseyside UFO Research Group (MUFORG), and by writers such as Christopher Evans (in *Cults of Unreason*) and Patrick Moore (in *Can You Speak Venusian?*). Even *Flying Saucer Review*, once friendly to the mystery when under the editorial control of Gordon Creighton rather than Charles Bowen, had turned against Shuttlewood and Warminster. However, for the UFO-friendly there is perhaps no smoke without fire, and the criticisms in mass market paperbacks such as those of Evans and Moore simply made more people curious.

But for how long would those people – and the new people that would be needed to sustain the human side of the phenomenon – remain curious? What could keep this nearly ten-year old unresolved mystery exciting and of interest?

End of Dreams - 1975-1980

The number of sightings at Warminster continued to decrease. Yet the skywatchers remained constant. 1976 was the peak of Steve's skywatching activity. He and his friends spent many nights of that glorious summer trekking around the hills. For Kevin, 1976 was the beginning of the skywatching experiences that were to lead to other, more interesting, events that he would later document in *UFO Warminster: Cradle of Contact*. We both remember that even in 1976, Cradle Hill continued to attract large groups of skywatchers. Their cars still snaked down the hill, parked up against the tall banks where the road had, over the years, formed a holloway.

By this time Arthur Shuttlewood had virtually retired from skywatching, because of ill-health. Occasionally, on warm summer nights, he was still to be found at his beloved Cradle Hill. Without his continuing presence and availability, the Warminster mystery lacked somebody who knew about the phenomenon, somebody to guide and inform new-comers to Warminster and the hills. It lacked a *figure-head*. In 1975, however, that was to change.

Fountains and Stars

In late 1975, Peter and Jane Paget opened a UFO research centre in Warminster. It was called the Fountain Centre, located in a house they called Star House. The house was a large, Victorian building that looked rather grand, but closer inspection revealed it to be in need of repairs. Surprisingly, despite Warminster's place in UFO history, the Fountain Centre was the first place of its type; it was intended to provide a focus for UFO studies and a place for curious visitors to the town to meet.

In 1976 the Fountain Centre also began to offer accommodation to visiting skywatchers. Star House had twenty-one rooms, including a separate three-roomed annexe that had once been the servants' quarters. The annexe had been converted into a self-catering apartment. The annexe was spartan, but comfortable enough; it also afforded, Kevin remembers, a certain amount of independence. He and his friend were the first to stay in the annexe when they visited in July 1976, and were possibly the first paying guests at Star House.

Star House and the Fountain Centre aimed to offer information, advice and shelter to those who came to Warminster to study the phenomena that had been seen and heard in and around the town. The house itself sat within extensive grounds, and the Pagets planned that the Fountain Centre should become a self-sufficient community within three years. Other plans included a holistic clinic and a large library that would provide books and journals covering all aspects of the paranormal and New Age beliefs.

The *Fountain Journal*, a quarterly magazine available only to subscribers, had been one of the Fountain Centre's earliest projects. The intention was that the magazine should contain the latest UFO reports, from Warminster and beyond, and information on a number of related paranormal subjects. Shuttlewood was to be the editor and chief contributor. With his help, the magazine had got off the ground far sooner than the Pagets had hoped – the first issue was published at Easter, 1976.

Peter Paget also wanted to set up regional branches of the Fountain Centre, to form a national network of UFO researchers. Each branch would be known as a Fountain Centre Association, and would bring together like-minded individuals within a particular region. Kevin and his friends were to set up one of the first such Associations, in the West Midlands.

However, within a few months of Kevin's visit, the Fountain Centre was in trouble. Issue 3 of the *Fountain Journal* contains a plea for financial assistance: 'Editorial (Fountain Centre in Danger!)'. Jane Paget's mother, Mrs. Margaret Tedder-Shepherd, had bought Star House with the Pagets – in fact, she had provided at least fifty percent of the equity. She had now withdrawn that financial support. Without it, the Pagets would be unable to continue with their plans for the Fountain Centre, at least at Star House. Nonetheless, even in the face of these financial difficulties, the Pagets were con-fident enough in their ambitious plans that they provided an outline of them in the fourth issue of the *Fountain Journal*. However, later issues of the *Fountain Journal* contained no editorials or articles announcing that the Fountain Centre had been saved.

The pages of the *Fountain Journal* reveal the continuing decline in local UFO sightings. As we noted at the begin-ning of this chapter, the number of visitors to the local hills appeared to be holding up, with groups of skywatchers, many of whom were regulars, gathering at

The Fountain Centre,

Star House,

78 Portway,

WARMINSTER,

Wilts.

Dear Friend,

This is to announce the setting-up of The Fountain Centre in
Warminster. We hope it will provide a long-felt need for all who
are genuinely interested in the existence of flying phenomena in
local skies, which constitute an aerial enigma throughout our
planet.

Whence do they originate? What are main aims, purposes and
intentions of this mysterious Intelligence? Quietly, without dis-
harmony or unnecessary bickering between extremist pseudoscientific or ultra-religious schools of thought and points of
view, we are hopeful of success in our quest for Truth.

The Fountain Centre believes that prompt mass-communication
is essential to bring about the advance of a common goal, having
an important bearing on the future of Mankind. To this end,
meetings of people sharing a healthy curiosity about matters
having Universal appeal and significance are obviously key
factors in resolving that quest . . .

Accommodation for sky-watchers will be available at Star
House, where The Fountain Centre will operate and be based. It
overlooks Elm Hill and Cop Heap, has views of rolling hills and
verdant dales leading to Cradle Hill and Cley Hill; and self-
catering facilities or bed-and-breakfast at reasonable terms may
be opted for by friends who visit a centre as refreshing to the
senses as its name . . .

Other advantages of a stay at Star House include study
projects for subscribers to the FOUNTAIN JOURNAL, a non-
secretarian publication enlivened by actual sighting accounts,
experiences, informed commentary and knowledgable articles,
envisaged to travel world-wide and be read in far-off parts of
our globe by fellow-devotees and questers for Truth. Up-to-date
happenings of the unusual at Warminster will be related therein
and continue to be a leading feature of its contents.

Healing and therapy, by utilizing the natural power of
Wiltshire county and countryside, will be an asset to the weary
in body, jaded in mind, sick in spirit. Added to which are
benefits of astrological advice on health and personality
problems in life. Also, important to the questing visitor, help-
ful guidance is readily on-the-spot regarding location, travel
arrangements and facilities for sky-watching sessions in the area.

We wish you well and - if you come - assure you of a
pleasant stay, which we trust will be visually rewarded. PLEASE
book well in advance of your visit. The quest is on - and will
rapidly continue . . .

Friends here are Peter and Jane Paget, and Arthur Shuttlewood.

88

weekends. However, judging by the contents of the *Fountain Journal*, those skywatchers weren't reporting many UFOs. Sightings from the people in the town had already fallen away by the end of the 1960s. Now, it seemed, the UFOs were no longer putting on a show even for the faithful.

Perhaps skywatchers were not too disappointed by the lack of action in the skies. The long, hot summer of 1976 probably helped sustain the numbers visiting Cradle Hill. It was certainly, as both authors remember, a perfect summer for skywatching, with honeyed sunsets, warm, clear nights, and beautiful, hazy lemon sunrises.

We noted earlier the increase in mass-market paperbacks related to UFOs. In this new market, even Arthur Shuttlewood was to find himself courted again by a mainstream publisher; Sphere released his *The Flying Saucerers* in November 1976. This book was a compendium of local, national and worldwide UFO sightings, and a smorgasbord of ufological theorising familiar to any student of UFO phenomena. The book was not as outlandish as *UFOs - Key to the New Age*, and seems to have excited the reading public enough to have been reprinted twice.

The Fountain Centre, Star House and the Pagets provided, at last, something, somebody, to replace Arthur Shuttlewood, who, as we have noted, had retired from skywatching. Shuttlewood had charisma, the slow countryman's drawl, the storytelling ability; but the Pagets provided something else: a direct connection between ufology and the New Age, holistic health, organic gardens, astrology readings, and so on. The connections, though perhaps not clear at the time, were later realised in such events as *The Mind Body Spirit Festival*, which first took place at the Olympia Exhibition Centre in London in 1977.

A Collapse at the Centre

How quickly a dream can turn to nightmare. The Pagets were successful in establishing themselves as the centre of ufology in Warminster. However, Shuttlewood, so happy to be part of the *Fountain Journal* when it had started, soon left the editorial board. Issue No.4 of the *Journal* notes that it is able to continue thanks to the financial assistance of Shuttlewood, but it appears that he no longer wanted anything to do with the content.

Initiated in late 1975, in financial trouble by Easter 1976, losing Shuttlewood – the authentic voice of the Warminster mystery – from the editorial board; the Fountain Centre did not appear to be built on solid foundations. Still, it staggered on into 1977. The Pagets told Kevin, when he visited during the Easter of 1977, that Star House was to be sold, but, as yet, they hadn't found a buyer. The financial support they had asked for had not been forthcoming.

If the *Fountain Journal* reported anything novel at all, outside of the steadily diminishing Warminster UFO reports, it was the experiments in contact involving Kevin and his group of friends, described in *UFO Warminster: Cradle of Contact*. The other scoop for the *Journal* had been the UFO sightings in Winchester, involving Ted Pratt and Joyce Bowles. Otherwise, the *Journal* appeared to grow thinner with every issue, and to be padded with articles on astrology by Jane Paget and short stories by Peter Paget.

At least the Thing was still putting in an appearance. Kevin, his friend Colin, and another skywatcher visited Cradle Hill one night during their Easter visit, and were rewarded with a sighting. They spotted a red light hovering over the West Wiltshire Golf Club situated on nearby Elm Hill. The light moved off towards Copheap, but then a second came over the horizon, soon followed by two others, all following the same path as the first. They flew in single file and the same distance apart. Their lights all flashed together, once every second. All the UFOs ended up hovering over Battlesbury Hill. There they stayed for five minutes; then each shot out a beam of light towards the ground. The first object then catapulted itself high into the sky at a fantastic rate. While still moving upwards at great speed, it executed a flawless 90 degree turn to the right without stopping.

Twelve minutes later, the remaining objects began a rapid ascent upwards, remaining in their formation, flashing regularly, until they disappeared from sight, never to be seen again that night. Throughout, the Things had remained silent.

UFO-INFO Exchange Library

Warminster was no longer – from a ufological point of view – a one-horse town. In 1977, UFO-INFO Exchange Library had been founded. This was the latest project to have the blessing of Arthur Shuttlewood. He was now an editor of the magazine, also called *UFO-INFO*, produced by this group. UFO-INFO was a connecting and networking organisation, dedicated to the free exchange of ufological information. They had 'offices' in Warminster, Trowbridge, and Weston-super-Mare. They were non-profit making, had no membership – and thus asked for no membership fee – and had no rules. They only requested that if a reader of the magazine had information about UFOs – written, or recorded on tape – that they pass it to UFO-INFO, who would catalogue it and disseminate it for use by other UFO organisations or ufologists.

Factional Friction

Having two UFO groups in town could only, to those who know their ufological history, mean trouble. That there was rivalry between the groups, Kevin can testify. Only in ufology can such a struggle commence over something of so little importance to the rest of the population. The Fountain Centre and the fledgling UFO-INFO were vying to become the 'official' voice of the town's UFO community. Kevin notes that Paget now seemed to have little credibility with the town's UFO researchers. Kevin recalls visiting John and Maureen Rowston, the Warminster-based officers of UFO-INFO:

> After the obligatory cup of tea, John outlined the situation. It appeared that Peter and Jane objected to another UFO research group in Warminster, as the Pagets felt they were best suited to the job in hand. [...] It had become clear to John that the Pagets [viewed] the subject as a way to make money. This, John and Maureen felt, was contrary to the spirit of UFO research, so had split with the Fountain Centre to help set up another organisation... This organisation would be non-profit, staffed by keen volunteers, and run by members in their spare time. It would publish a quarterly magazine, *UFO-Info*, which would be sent to subscribers. The only money they would receive would be that required to cover costs, such as postage and packing, or to buy cassette tapes. If any money was left over, it was to be ploughed back into

the organisation, not squandered on luxuries... (*UFO Warminster: Cradle of Contact*, p.110)

John Rowston went on to explain that Shuttlewood had become disillusioned with the Fountain Centre, and was now involved with UFO-INFO, the ideals and principles of which appealed to him. He had offered to become their chief spokesman and to champion their cause.

Out of this World

The BBC approached the subject of UFOs again in 1977. Arthur Shuttlewood had been invited to take part. The programme, titled *Out of this World*, was broadcast on May 10th, 1977. Kevin had been informed of the documentary via the Pagets at the Fountain Centre. The BBC had assured everyone who was to take part that the documentary was to be a frank, critical, unsensational look at the subject. Kevin and his friends hoped it would show that ufologists and skywatchers weren't the cranks they were made out to be by the popular press.

Unfortunately, it was not to be. Although the BBC spent two nights filming on Cradle Hill, interviewing Arthur Shuttlewood and other skywatchers, the edited programme contained only a two minute segment about Warminster. For those two minutes, the editors had selected Shuttlewood's most outlandish stories.

The Warminster mystery was still of interest to the media, but only, it seemed, to be then treated derisively or dismissively. Warminster's appearance in the documentary did nothing to encourage skywatchers or UFOs back to the town.

9.55 Out of this World

A housewife in Staffordshire saw two space-suited men looking down at her from a huge metallic disc. A peasant in Brazil reported being taken into a spacecraft, and was later said to be suffering from exposure to radiation. Hundreds of similar accounts have come in from all over the world and many theories have been advanced about what is going on. In tonight's documentary, **Hugh Burnett** talks to some of the people who have seen strange things and others who have been puzzling over what, to them, is a very alarming phenomenon.

FEATURE P4

Film editor DON FAIRSERVICE
Producer HUGH BURNETT

The Fountain Centre Closes

By August 1977, a buyer had been found for Star House. Originally, the Pagets had planned to remain in Warminster, moving to a smaller house while carrying out what they had planned for the Fountain Centre. By now, however, and as hinted at in the pages of the *Fountain Journal*, other excitements were tempting the Pagets. The *Fountain Journal* had contained reports of the UFO sightings in a quiet corner of the Pembrokeshire countryside, around the Haverfordwest area, a phenomenon that was to become known in UFO research circles as the 'Dyfed Enigma'. It was this that now appeared to interest Peter Paget. He had, it seems, exhausted his research into the Warminster mystery. Now an 'expert' on the subject of UFOs – thanks to his experiences in Warminster – he intended moving to Wales and exploring this new UFO phenomenon.

By 1978, the Fountain Centre had closed, and the Pagets had decamped to Pembrokeshire. Ironically, in the middle of 1977, UFO reports had flooded into the Centre, and requests for membership of the Association ran at an all-time high. Why? Because the Centre had been featured in the widely read national Sunday newspaper, the *News of the World*, in the spring of 1977. Yet, despite this upsurge in sighting reports, despite this enthusiasm for the Fountain Centre, still the Pagets left town.

Reasons to be Cheerless

The Fountain Journal, No. 11 of 1977, had been the final edition of the magazine. In it, an editorial by Peter Paget, entitled 'The Good, the Bad, and the Ugly', attempted to explain – in his own inimitable style – why the Fountain Centre was being closed:

> Old friends who will have been with us for some time will recall the ups and downs of the centre as hinted at in the Journal. These reflect the progress and the setbacks that we have journeyed through since the early days of our beginning in 1975. People, time and projects have come and gone, results achieved, policies changed, the world changing with every turn, lessons learnt and so to move on.

The Pagets claimed to have:

> made tremendous advances in our understanding of the world in which we live, the other worlds in space and time and their relationship to this beautiful but sorry planet.

Unfortunately, however, while trying to compartment-alise the knowledge they had gained, and only releasing particular information to particular participants according to the Fountain Centre's structure, the Pagets had:

> come under constant and severe attack. Who seeks to know must first prove to be wise enough to be given knowledge and know when not to use it. The exoteric is always fighting to invade and take over the esoteric. This it can never do for it does not perceive the nature of the division necessary.
>
> There is of course another faction who fear knowledge by virtue of their position of ignorance, misguided belief, or because it would affect their 'superior' position.

The attempt to control the release of information had led to such enmity that Peter Paget was claiming that his legal advisers had informed him "action could be effectively taken against certain identified elements who have not only broken the civil but also the criminal laws", although he had decided not to take this approach. However, because of these problems the Fountain Centre had been forced to into a reappraisal "of its long term position, security and deployment of funds". It had closed its doors to all-comers. Information services were to be limited to members of Fountain Centre Associations. The *Fountain Journal* was to continue, operating from Warminster. The Fountain Centre Associations, such as the one Kevin and his friends ran in the West Midlands, would each create their own newsletter, and would be run and financed by their own members. Meanwhile, the "inner circle of the Fountain Centre" was to continue "as an esoteric organisation".

Of course, the *Fountain Journal* never continued. What happened to the Fountain Centre Associations is unclear. If the Fountain Centre was ever heard of again, it must have only been in Pembrokeshire. Certainly Kevin, for whom the Fountain Centre had become central to his experiences, never heard from Paget again. Despite nurturing the 'alien' contacts established by Kevin and his friends, Paget had nothing more to do with them:

> Although the Pagets had promised to keep in touch, they never did. Colin remembers bitterly that after we left the town [at the end of our visit] we never saw or heard from them again. (*UFO Warminster*, p.95)

Where Have All the UFOs Gone...

So, with the Pagets gone, muttering about the esoteric and the exoteric and abandoning contactees they had helped nurture, UFO-INFO was left as the only ufological organisation in town. The way was clear for them to remain the voice of the local ufological fraternity, exchanging exciting local UFO reports with other UFO groups, at the centre of lines of communication that would connect, in Vallee's term, the Invisible College.

And yet, UFO-INFO appears to have lasted little longer than the Fountain Centre. The last magazine we have is Volume 2, Number 2, of June 1978. UFO-INFO staggered on for a few months after the last edition of the magazine, replacing it instead with something more in the way of a pamphlet. However, as the magazine was an integral part of the group's *raison d'etre*, one of the vehicles through which the exchange of information was enabled, it is hard to imagine how a magazine-less UFO-INFO could have survived.

In the space of a few months, then, both the Fountain Centre and UFO-INFO had collapsed. The only voice left to proselytise Warminster was Arthur Shuttlewood, too frail now to skywatch. Indeed, when the curious called at Shuttlewood's home, the door would normally be answered by either his wife on one of his sons. This was done to protect Shuttlewood from the more extreme elements of ufology.

If ufologists were still visiting the hills, they were reporting very little, as indicated by the contents of both the *Fountain Journal* and *UFO-INFO*. The slope of the imaginary graph of UFOs over time was accelerating ever-downwards. Even the numbers of skywatchers was diminishing. The Warminster mystery – already elided in ufological annals as some weird aberration that should not be taken seriously – was in the process of being forgotten. Time, then, for two more books from Shuttlewood.

UFO Magic in Motion and *More UFOs Over Warminster*

Shuttlewood managed to produce two more books on UFOs before falling silent: a mass-market paperback published by Sphere, *UFO Magic in Motion*, and the hardback *More UFOs Over Warminster*. *UFO Magic in Motion* follows the same path as *The Flying Saucerers*; it contains reports of local, national, and international UFO sightings, and more speculative theorising. The local reports include sightings up until 1976. Many of the reports appear to have been collected during Shuttlewood's involvement with the Pagets and UFO-INFO. Steve knows that one of the sightings reported in the book was reported by him to the Fountain Centre, and, in a coincidental twist of fate, actually written down by Kevin when *he* was staying at Star House! *More UFOs Over Warminster* is more of the same; local, national and international UFO sightings, this time including reports up until 1978. There is slightly less theoretical speculation in this book than in earlier books, although there is a divagation into ley-lines. What is interesting is that, in this book, Shuttlewood says, "I honestly think that the majority of UFOs are inherently of our native planet". (*More UFOs Over Warminster*, p.148) After fourteen years, Shuttlewood is moving away from his long-held belief that the UFOs are the craft of extra-terrestrials. Yes, he only thinks the majority of UFOs are of this planet, which still enables a percentage to be not of this world; after all, he has been contacted by the Aenstrians, who were not from this *cantel*. Wherever they are from, however, the UFOs are:

> of universal importance and significance. They have probably been on Earth since before the germination of Man; and maybe long, long ago, when UFOnauts were in purely physical form as we are today, they even begat us unto the wonderful, mighty Universe. (*More UFOs Over Warminster*, p.151).

Time to Die

The hippie era was over. Punk and new wave music had established itself. The hills were now empty, apart from a few die-hards. UFO sightings in Warminster had dried up. The phenomena that had started in the early hours of Christmas Day 1964 had, after 14 years, finally fallen silent, had finally dimmed. The Warminster mystery was being ignored in ufological studies, a madness best forgotten. Now, at last, Shuttlewood was quiet, no longer embarrassing *serious* ufology. Researchers could move on to the really *real* incidents, like Rendlesham, and Cosford, and Bonnybridge, and Rendlesham again. Warminster could be forgotten, mentioned only in passing in histories of ufology.

The Warminster Triangle 1981 Onwards

The Warminster mystery had, according to most ufological histories, petered out by the early 1970s. Dewey and Ries, in *In Alien Heat: The Warminster Mystery Revisited*, and Goodman, in *UFO Warminster: Cradle of Contact*, show that the phenomenon continued well into the late 1970s. As we described in the previous chapter, it wasn't even until the middle 1970s that UFO groups were established in Warminster. However, it is true that interest in Warminster, among ufologists and sky-watchers, dramatically tailed off after 1977. This can be seen in Kevin's *UFO Warminster*, where his later visits to Cradle Hill no longer coincide with large gatherings of skywatchers, and tend to be made only in the company of his friends.

What is also obvious from *UFO Warminster*, from the UFO newsletters and magazines, and from the personal experiences of Steve and Kevin, is that UFO sightings had also dramatically decreased. Among the reasons for this, we surmise, are that:

- The numbers of skywatchers at Cradle, Starr and Cley Hills continued the slow decline already evident at the beginning of the decade.

- Some skywatchers no longer visited the local hills intent on witnessing wonders, but had become inherently more sceptical.

- Arthur Shuttlewood and his "team" of skywatchers no longer regularly visited Cradle Hill.

- The interest of other UFO groups in Warminster had decreased – whether through scepticism, cynicism, or Warminster-fatigue – meaning that information from Warminster was less likely to be promulgated to other ufologists and those curious about UFOs, and thus Warminster was less likely to be visited and UFO sightings made.

People were still aware of the Warminster mystery, and people still visited the town hoping to see or hear something. Timothy Green Beckley, a ufologist from the United States, visited Cradle Hill in 1981. He had been invited by the Earl of Clancarty, Brinsley Le Poer Trench, to speak at the House of Lords to a special group, drawn from both Houses of Parliament, that had been organised "to get to the bottom of the UFO mystery". When Green Beckley arrived in Warminster, he went out for a meal with Shuttlewood and Bob Strong, and then visited Cradle Hill in their company, where they also met some other skywatchers. During the skywatch they caught sight of and signalled to a light in the sky that appeared to respond, before rain forced them down from the hill.*

---

* Personal email to Kevin Goodman

The Warminster Triangle is Published

Ken Rogers, skywatcher, ufologist, and former member of Contact UK, died in 1993. Rogers had been a vocal proponent of the Warminster mystery, and was a link to the days of Shuttlewood, skywatches, mimeographed newsletters, and to the general excitement of the Warminster UFO flap. With his death, a thread in the web of the Warminster mystery was broken. He left all his notes and research about the Thing and other phenomena to the local museum.

Before his death, Rogers had been writing a book on the Warminster mystery; this was to be posthumously published in 1994. Titled *The Warminster Triangle,* the book is, essentially, a list of UFO sightings from Warminster, culled from the pages of Shuttlewood's books and Rogers' own files. Indeed, Rogers includes in his book an acknowledgement to Shuttlewood, saying that *The Warminster Triangle* is published "in tribute to Arthur Shuttlewood" and his "vastly underrated contribution to UFO studies".

However, he also notes in his book that "towards the end of the 1970s the frequency of strange happenings in the Warminster Triangle appeared to peter out". (*The Warminster Triangle,* p.198) Such was the paucity of UFO sightings after 1981 that Rogers' book, published in 1994, only includes one UFO report after that date. The event reported is typical for Warminster. At about 1 a.m. in the morning on January 23rd, 1988, a CB enthusiast visiting the downs above Westbury describes how first his CB radio equipment failed, then his car ignition. The witness then heard a hum, and a light slowly enveloped his vehicle. The light increased in intensity, remained at

UFO expert's gift to town

UFO expert Ken Rogers who died in January has left thousands of pounds to Warminster in his will.

Mr Rogers, of The Avenue, died on January 15 after a long illness. aged 44. His gift to the town is expected to be between £40,000 and £70,000.

Books and manuscripts from Mr Rogers' research into the famous Warminster Thing have been left to the Dewey Museum. He first came to the town in the 1960s as a Daily Express reporter researching sightings of the local UFO and decided later to settle in Warminster. Museum staff are currently sifting through the material he collected.

Most of the money will go towards the upkeep of the obelisk in Silver Street. with the consent of Warminster Town Council. A plaque recording the obelisk's history and stating that maintenance is carried out in Mr Roger's memory is also to be erected.

Another plaque will be put up at the Rainbow End Inn, Steeple Langford. to record its history.

The balance of the money will help maintain local rights of way and help fund other matters of local history and interest at the trustees' discretion.

its most intense for about ten seconds, before slowly attenuating and disappearing. The man, "terrified", Rogers writes, "tried the ignition again, and it worked, upon which he left at once for home". (*The Warminster Triangle*, p.160)

As to the triangle, Rogers notes that it is:

> A mystery zone in Wessex where strange unaccountable events by day and night, and the ever increasing strange circles that appear in crop fields, have affected thousands of people, particularly since the 1960s. No one can say for sure where the affectionate, catchy name came from. (*The Warminster Triangle*, 'Introduction')

The triangle has its baseline from Warminster to Winchester, and its apex at Wantage. Rogers notes that others have placed the Warminster corner further west, at Glastonbury. Wherever the corners of this triangle are, Warminster is a part of it, and, with its dramatic and numerous UFO sightings, seems to have provided the triangle's appellation.

Crop Circles

The tagline of Ken Rogers' book is 'Astounding UFO and Crop Circle Sightings'. Despite this, there is little mention of crop circles, beyond noting that they were now occurring within Rogers' triangle. In the years after Ken Rogers' death, crop circles and Warminster were more often mentioned in the same breath. If the Warminster mystery had faded into the background, it hadn't been totally forgotten. It remained in the collective memory of ufologists and the folklore of the area. Thus, when crop circles began to appear in Wiltshire in the late 1980s and early 1990s, an association was quickly forged between the older Warminster mystery and the new phenomenon.

Certainly, Wiltshire was host to many of the crop circles reported when that phenomenon first started to appear. For Rogers, the proximity of Warminster to Avebury and the number of crop-circles falling within the area he identified as The Warminster Triangle were significant. Interestingly, the International Crop Circle Database (http://ccdb.cropcircleresearch.com/index.cgi, accessed 20/06/11) only reports eight crop circles within a few miles of Warminster itself. Thus, the connection between Warminster and crop circles is, to us, best described as tenuous. However, the connection, the meme, is out there, and a web search using Google will reveal instances where Warminster and crop circles remain linked.

Hooten and the Faulkner Photo

The Faulkner photograph had for a long time remained the iconic image of the Warminster mystery. Whatever else had been said and written about the Warminster mystery, Faulkner's 'eye in the sky', as Shuttlewood had called it, kept on staring back, daring you to call it out.

Many people had, of course, assumed the photograph to be a hoax, but as with all well-executed hoaxes, proving that the artefact is not what it claims to be can be difficult. What clues are there, after all, in the Faulkner photograph itself that could help us judge the reality of his story?

There have been suggestions over the years that the photograph is a hoax. In 1992, John Spencer of BUFORA interviewed Roger Hooten, who had been a compositor on the *Warminster Journal* at the time the Faulkner story was published, and claimed to have knowledge that the picture was a hoax. This interview was published in *BUFORA Times*, later in that year.

In 1994, Roger Hooten – who had been a compositor at the *Warminster Journal* in the 1960s – also sent a letter to the *Daily Mirror*, and to the *Journal*, again claiming that Faulkner's photograph was a hoax. Hooten's story is covered in detail in Dewey and Ries's *In Alien Heat*, and in Clarke and Roberts *Flying Saucerers*. We will only adumbrate the story here. Hooten claims that the Faulkner photograph and story were created as a practical joke to be played on Charles Mills, the *Journal*'s editor, and to, as Andy Roberts puts it, "inject mischief into Warminster's rapidly developing UFO mythos". (Clarke and Roberts, *Flying Saucerers*, p.150) The practical joke was created by Hooten, Faulkner, and some other friends. Faulkner's photograph and accompanying report of the sighting was sent to the *Journal* in the form of a letter, which was subsequently published in the 'Letters to the Editor' column of the *Journal*; there had been a long-established tradition at the *Journal* of placing prank letters in this column. Shuttlewood took the photograph to the *Daily Mirror*, where it and the accompanying story were turned into a double-page spread, and published on the same day as the *Journal*, much to the consternation of Charles Mills, the *Journal*'s editor.

Faulkner denied Hooten's story, while never quite saying that the photograph was of a UFO. "I maintain that the photograph I took is completely genuine", he said in the *Western Daily Press* (18th April, 1994). Faulkner also claimed that he'd never heard of Hooten before Hooten's letter to the *Journal*.

In 2005, Faulkner again claimed that his image was "an authentic photograph of a UFO". This assertion was made in an email to Steve Dewey, after Faulkner had requested sight of the draft version of Dewey and Ries's *In Alien Heat* when they had asked permission for his photograph to be used. *In Alien Heat* contains an alternative account of the creation of the photograph to that provided by Hooten. Unknown to Steve, one of his friends, Will Bonner, had once been a housemate of Faulkner's. Bonner recalled that during the time he and Faulkner had lived together Faulkner had once, during a conversation about the Warminster UFO mystery, stated that the photograph had been a joke that had run out of control. (For more details, see *In Alien Heat*, pp.158-160)

We have been in touch with Faulkner while preparing this book, and he has provided us with an interesting recollection that explains how Steve's friend Will might have misremembered events; we include it in full, as requested by Faulkner, for the sake of completeness during this anniversary year. Much of this will only make complete sense if you have read *In Alien Heat*, or Robert's and Clarke's *Flying Saucerers*. In this statement, Faulkner once again states that he never knew Roger Hooten, who claimed to have been part of the hoax in 1965. Here is the account:

> Will Bonner was my brother-in law from August 1977 until late 1984. In September 1977 he prevailed upon his sister (my wife at the time) to provide him with somewhere to live and so we made room for him in our rented flat in Leek, Staffordshire. I also found him a job with my employer Hawkesworth Skysports, a local

business that imported Wills Wing hang gliders from the USA in kit form and also operated a flight training school for this type of aircraft.

The story told by Will Bonner regarding my Thing photograph is false but tallies exactly with a conversation that occurred during a social evening I spent together with my wife at The Herbage Farm, home of my employer and friend Malcolm Hawkesworth. Will Bonner and several hang glider pilots and their girlfriends were also present. During the evening the subject of my photograph came up and inevitably the 'ribbing' soon began. Unsurprisingly, being accused of faking the photograph was not a new experience for me and I didn't take offence, I never have done, in fact it's only to be expected. Anyway a very good humoured and speculative discussion began which was focused on how such a hoax, if indeed it was one, could have been achieved. Sometime previously I had loaned Malcolm my copy of Arthur Shuttlewood's book 'The Warminster Mystery' so he was familiar with the reported sequence of events in the town. I seem to recall that Malcolm and Alan Hetherington, one of the other hang glider pilots present, led the theorising. Will Bonner may have made a contribution to the discussion although I don't recall it. Obviously he remembered some of the speculation voiced at the time.

I'd like to correct an important detail. The original Daily Mirror report stated that I was taking the camera to my mother's house for my sister to borrow. That has been repeated in several subsequent publications but in fact I was bringing the camera back after my sister had used it. It was a 35millimetre camera containing (I think) a 24-frame film, although it may have been a 36-frame. The film was developed and printed at a photographers in Warminster; I can't recall the name of the shop but remember it being opposite the Methodist church. At no point was any developing or printing carried out in Westbury. The object I photographed was only a very small speck on the print. The rest of the prints were of my sister and friends at a college party of some kind with her fellow students. That was the purpose of loaning her my camera but those prints were of no interest to me. I gave them and the negative strip to her but kept the Thing print and negative and took it to the same photographer in Warminster to be enlarged. That enlargement is the one first shown in the Warminster Journal and Daily Mirror, and a number of publications since.

I want to repeat my assertions that I didn't know and have never met or communicated in any manner with Roger Hooten. And I did not meet or know Bill Newton, my sister's future husband until 1968, some three years after the Thing photograph was published.

Finally, and as has been pointed out frequently in the past, it is often difficult to prove that a photograph is a fake, but by the same token it is even more difficult to prove that it isn't.

However, Hooten's story, first published by BUFORA in 1992, and then given wider coverage through national media in 1994, was a reminder of what Warminster had once been. The next reminder was not to be controversial, but tinged with sadness.

The Passing of an Era

In 1996, with controversy over Faulkner's photograph still rumbling in the background, Arthur Shuttlewood died. His passing was mourned by the ufologists and skywatchers who remembered his involvement in a mystery central to their lives. With his death, those who might have forgotten about the mystery were reminded of it, with obituaries appearing in *The Warminster Journal* and *Fortean Times*. Thus, at the same time as an era ended, memories of that era were rekindled by Shuttlewood's passing.

50 years of UFOs

Shuttlewood had died just as the Warminster mystery was re-emerging, blinking, from the shadows. In the 1990s, UFO books once again began to mention the dread word *Warminster* – often dismissively. John Spencer's *Gifts of the Gods* (1994) covers the Warminster phenomenon in a paragraph. David and Therese Marie Barclay's *UFOs: The Final Answer (1993)* gives it but a line. Patrick Harpur's *Daimonic Reality* (1994) describes, in the space of a paragraph, Shuttlewood as a shaman. Peter Brookesmith's *UFO: The Complete Sightings Catalogue* (1995) devotes a small section to the Thing in the chapter *Abductions and Absurdities*. Finally, in *UFO 1947-1997: A Definitive History of the UFO Phenomenon* (1997), edited by Hilary Evans and Dennis Stacey, John Rimmer, a critic of the Warminster mystery but also a long-standing observer of it, was at last given an entire chapter to remember the Warminster mystery, and to discuss what had happened.

In Alien Heat and *UFO Warminster*

The first full-length, in-depth re-examination and re-appraisal of the Warminster mystery was Dewey and Ries's *In Alien Heat: The Warminster Mystery Revisited* (2005). At least one reason for writing the book was to reintroduce the Warminster mystery to an audience of ufologists that had, at the time of the book's publication, by now forgotten Warminster's place in ufological history. Just before completion of *In Alien Heat*, however,

Death Of Arthur Shuttlewood

Arthur Shuttlewood, who brought the eyes of the world to Warminster and its UFOs, died peacefully at Warminster Hospital on Thursday last week.

His funeral arrangements were carried out by his son Glen, the Portway funeral director. The funeral was held on Wednesday afternoon at the Minster Church, conducted by the Revd Glenn Coggins and Roger Snarpe.

He was a much-loved husband, father, grandfather and great-grandfather.

Daily Mirror report started the imagination of lots of people. They went up on Cley Hill and other vantage points for all-night vigils, to wait and see what would come out of the night sky.

Arthur Shuttlewood was the journalist on the ... newspaper in the 1950s, when his imagination was fired by the news that Unidentified Flying Objects had landed, or been seen, or were maybe hovering around Warminster.

It became a cause celebre, as his ... His writings fuelled the controversy, and copies of his books can still be found on bookshelves round the town.

Arthur Shuttlewood with the late Lord Bath, pointing out the spot where the UFO was sighted. Later he wrote about 'astounding UFO sightings'.

News Talent And Devotion

I first started to come across Arthur Shuttlewood when finding bits of yesterday's news for the Journal's Days of Yore, 25 years ago, which then took us back to the Sixties, writes Anna Schott.

If you can imagine stories beginning like this, 'A Warminster man has been having vivid nightmares lately – dreaming that pulpy green monsters are going to invade his home and batter his bedroom door in a squashed multitude...' – for an article about a hobby gardener who grows cucumbers on a single knuckle – then you have an idea of Arthur Shuttlewood's talent for making a moderately interesting story special.

Who was writing this? I asked. Who was he then?

It was Mr. Shuttlewood, writing for the Journal throughout the Sixties and well into the next decade.

I was charmed by this talent and his devotion to look so sadly at the local ...

Later I realised this was also the man who gave Warminster a running chronology of The Thing, first as a reporter on the paper, then in his books – which made his chosen town famous as a UFO centre.

I treasure my copies of The Warminster Mystery and Warnings from Flying Friends.

'They're like gold dust now', said close associate in the days of The Thing, the late Ken Rogers, to me some years ago.

You want bizarre? You want the Fifes? It's nothing in comparison with that profile of Shuttlewood's encounters with that ...

Warnings

... Sky used to ring him from a phonebox in Boreham Field.

If it wasn't true, it was truly well invented, and I don't really care either way.

Those warnings from flying friends, whoever they were, were deeply touching and full of wisdom, written by someone who had lived through a world war: 'Learn to live fully and not fragmentally. Thus curing spiritual and mental and bodily ailments, they told him.

And, reflected Arthur, humanity is being threatened by its own creations, because spiritual and social sciences have not sufficiently progressed to allow us to determine uses to which their then important creations should be put.

there came a bombshell that necessitated some hurried rewriting; this bombshell is described in the next section.

A short while after the publication of *In Alien Heat*, Steve Dewey was contacted by Kevin Goodman to discuss a book he was writing that was later to become *UFO Warminster: Cradle of Contact* (2006). Despite Steve's 'hyper-scepticism', he was more than happy to help Kevin shape his book, and to provide editing assistance. Kevin's book describes the UFOs he saw while visiting Cradle Hill in the 1970s, and the "contacts" he and his friends made with an entity named Lenston. These events had been mentioned before, in *The Fountain Journal*, in Shuttlewood's later books, and in Rogers' *The Warminster Triangle*. *UFO Warminster*, however, was the first time the events had been related by Kevin, and contextualised with Kevin's lapsed Catholicism, his teen-age idealism, and so on. *UFO Warminster* also contained information on the UFO groups that existed in Warminster at the time, and on their rivalries, an aspect of the Warminster mystery that had never been discussed before.

Holten's Letter to the *Warminster Journal*

As we noted in an earlier chapter, David Holton plays a large part in the early stages of the Warminster mystery. He sent letters to the *Warminster Journal*, provided stories about unusual phenomena to Shuttlewood, and appeared in the media. As described more fully in Dewey and Ries's *In Alien Heat*, David Holton is absolutely central to the Warminster mystery. He is pivotal in changing one strange phenomenon – the noises reported around the town – into another – UFOs.

In the 10th June, 2005, edition of the *Warminster Journal*, a letter appeared that confirmed the suspicions of Dewey and Ries, and provided more information about Holton's involvement. Written by Holton, the letter claimed that he had intended to set in motion "a psychological experiment". The experiment, he says, "succeeded beyond even the wildest flight of my imagination". He even suggested that the Warminster Mystery be renamed the Crockerton Mystery, after the village in which he lived. Holton had studied hypnosis to help him in his job as a chiropodist, and as a result of those studies had become interested in mass hypnosis. When Shuttlewood began to report the strange sounds heard in late 1964 and early 1965, he was interested in the idea "that the public mood of the time was yearning for some demonstration of the unseen realms [*sic*] presence". He thus invented some stories – including the sorry tale of the demise of the flock of pigeons at Five Ash Lane – and sent them to the *Journal*. He felt that the subsequent sudden explosive growth in UFO sightings confirmed his thesis. Should we be in any doubt as to his belief in the ETH, or his role as a ufologist in the 'academic' sense, he says in his letter, "What, of course, is unbelievable are modern myths about flying saucers and other objects, crop circles and space aliens".

Can we believe Holton's "confession"? Well, Holton did provide Shuttlewood with stories about UFO sightings, and, as Shuttlewood notes, "It was Mr. Holton who first advanced the spacecraft theory and brought forth the killed pigeons evidence". (*The Warminster Myst-*

ery, p.85) Holton makes 'leading' predictions to Shuttle-wood, such as "there will be plenty of sightings in the future … Landings may have taken place already", as well as sending letters to the *Journal*, appearing in interviews on local TV, and so on. Interestingly, in the statement from which the above quote is taken, Holton says that, after this "prediction", he intends to wash his hands of the subject altogether, and that talk of an invasion is "utter rot". (*The Warminster Mystery*, p.85) Additionally, his belief in the power of hypnotism fits well with his attachment to alternative therapies such as herbalism and homeopathy. It is therefore highly likely that he had studied hypnotism, and was interested (or wary) of its power and abuses in the hands of advertising and religion.

Finally, it should be noted that Holton only appears in the narrative of *The Warminster Mystery* up until Shuttlewood's description of the public meeting. It is almost as if, from Holton's point of view, his job had been done; the Warminster mystery was by then capable of sustaining itself.

Weird and the Skywatches

The Warminster mystery was, it seems, popping its head above the parapet again. David Clarke and Andy Roberts devoted a full chapter to the phenomena in their *Flying Saucerers: A Social History of UFOlogy* (2007). Dewey and Ries's *In Alien Heat* and Goodman's *UFO Warminster* received favourable reviews in such publications as the *Fortean Times* and the *Warminster Journal*. While Steve is media-shy, Kevin has discussed Warminster on numerous local radio shows and television programmes, including UFO documentaries, and as a talking-head insert on the BBC's antiques show *Flog It* when it visited Warminster in 2009.

There was, anyway, something in the water, as they say. Warminster was by now, of course, a suitable case for nostalgia – along with hippies, flares, and Austin Allegros – and the first decade of the new century also saw interest in and nostalgia for the 1970s appearing in the media. For example, Jonathon Coe's *Rotter's Club* was published in 2001 (also adapted for television in 2005) and the BBC's *Life on Mars* was first broadcast in 2006.

Kevin in particular has always been keen to keep the memory of the Warminster mystery alive; in part because of what he experienced in Warminster, and in part to remember and relive the sense of community engendered by skywatches. *Keep the flame burning*, as he likes to say. To this end, he re-initiated organised skywatches at Cradle Hill in 2007. These have continued, and attract as many as 30-50 people. In 2009 and 2010, the Weird Paranormal Conference was held at Warminster's Athenaeum Centre. At both conferences, there were reminders of Warminster's past with Kevin Goodman speaking about the history of the mystery, and his experiences in the town. A skywatch then followed each conference, enabling the curious to experience an evening on Cradle Hill. The skywatches will probably continue for as long as Kevin can stand up.

Sightings Continue

And what of the UFOs themselves? Where do they fit into this renewed interest in and nostalgia for the mystery? Have they come out to play, nostalgic themselves? Have the Aenstrians revisited to check out the old telephone boxes?

The thing is that the Things never really went away. There has always been a continuing background of UFO sightings even while the world ignored Warminster. These sightings are now rarely reported in the *Warminster Journal*, and there is no longer a Shuttlewood, Rogers or Paget to document them; for example:

- The *Melksham Star* of the 5th March 1998 reported that the Koob children – Sarah, Kayli, and Yan – saw a silver and cigar-shaped UFO, shining like a mirror, hovering over their house in July 1997. A photograph that accompanied the story in the *Melksham Star* showed the young Koobs looking into the sky in front of Cley Hill.

- On November 16th, 2006, at about 4.45pm, a woman from Wanstrow, near Frome, reported seeing approximately six bright lights in the direction of Cley Hill making different patterns. Then, for about 30 seconds a triangular shape appeared. The sighting lasted for about 5 minutes. The military, police and the nearby Centre Parcs resort were contacted about the incident, but no explanation was forthcoming.

UFO Spotted Over Warminster

Two red lights were seen dancing in the night sky above Warminster before they disappeared into the distance, last month, said a town resident.

Mr. Malcolm Smith of Boreham Field said "It was a clear night at approximately ten minutes past eight o'clock and I was in my garden facing towards the North when I saw the lights very close together, possibly belonging to the same object.

"They were moving very erratically northwards, tumbling through the sky. I observed it for approximately 30 seconds until it disappeared from view near the horizon."

Mr. Smith, who has a degree in environmental science, added that it did not look like any terrestrial aircraft that he knew of. He has seen two other UFOs in the past three years, both in broad daylight.

This is just one of a long line of unexplained sightings reported to have been seen over the skies above Warminster in the last few decades.

Back to the Future

The Warminster mystery, which had been hidden for so long, has now re-emerged, and has been restored to its place in the history of British ufology. So with interest in Warminster reawakened, what next? We hope that there will be further re-analysis of the mystery, and that further stories will emerge. There is more, we believe, to be discovered about hoaxing in the area, more about the rivalry between the UFO groups, more about Shuttlewood, more about Rogers and Paget, more about the people who visited the hills and made the Warminster mystery what it was. Perhaps more will be discovered about other actors in the mystery as contacts are made and networks extended.

We hope that researchers do not continue to ignore the mystery, do not pass it off as a mad fad, but recognise it for what it was, what it represented, what it meant to particular groups of people, how it corresponded to and subsequently moulded other myths. We hope that when looking at other UFO flaps, other UFO cases, researchers recognise the mechanisms that propelled Warminster into the ufological spotlight.

We expect UFO sightings to continue.

Kevin Goodman and Steve Dewey

Bibliography

Introduction

This chapter lists the most important books mentioned in this book. We have split this chapter into the following sections:

- Currently available books that solely describe the Warminster mystery, or some aspect of it

- Out of print books that solely describe the Warminster mystery, or some aspect of it

- Currently available books that have a chapter about or an in-depth discussion of the Warminster mystery

- Out of print books that have a chapter about or an in-depth discussion of the Warminster mystery

There are other books that mention the Warminster mystery in passing; we refer you to the UFO-Warminster website for details of these books:

http://www.ufo-warminster.co.uk/books/books_other.htm

Books Solely About the Mystery

Current

In Alien Heat: The Warminster Mystery Revisited

Steve Dewey and John Ries

San Antonio and New York: Anomalist Books, 2005

Introduces the Warminster phenomenon to a new generation of readers. It contains a short history of the phenomenon, places it in its social and historical context, and examines the possible mechanisms that initiated and sustained this remarkable UFO flap.

UFO Warminster: Cradle of Contact

Kevin Goodman and Steve Dewey

Devon: Fortean Words, 2012

The author and a group of friends began to visit Warminster during the mid-1970s. They went to there to research the UFO sightings. Soon, they were to be the focus of the very phenomena they were researching. This is their story.

Conclusions From Controlled UFO Hoaxes

David Simpson

London: ICR, 2005

A monograph, derived from a seminar at the Institute of Cultural Research, that describes the various hoaxes performed by the Society for the Investigation of UFO Phenomena (SIUFOP) around Warminster, and the conclusions that can be drawn from them.

Note: Available directly from the Institute for Cultural Research

Out of Print

The Warminster Mystery

Arthur Shuttlewood

HB: London: Neville Spearman, 1968
PB: London: Tandem, 1973, repr. 1975

The dramatic description of the how the Warminster UFO sightings began, with witness accounts of strange "things" seen by day and night and disturbing sounds, and reports of conversations with the Aenstrians.

Warnings from Flying Friends

Arthur Shuttlewood

Warminster: Portway Press, 1968

An "important contribution" to the serious literature on flying mysteries, includes the sighting reports, theorising, and a description of the meeting with Aenstrian, Karne.

UFOs: Key to the New Age

Arthur Shuttlewood

London: Regency Press, 1971

The third and final book in what has become known as the "Warminster trilogy". Shuttlewood thought, at the time, that this would be his final book on the Warminster Mystery. This is a book that is mostly theorising, connected by reports of UFO sightings, a "gateway and entrance to new dimensions in universal thought and existence".

The Flying Saucerers

Arthur Shuttlewood

London: Sphere Books, 1977

"UFOs over rural England!" The book "examines numerous eye-witness accounts, relates chilling personal experiences, and provides strong evidence for extraterrestrial life".

UFO Magic in Motion

Arthur Shuttlewood

London: Sphere Books, 1979

Shuttlewood's "most penetrating study yet of a phenomenon which has captured the imagination of millions of people", the book describes local and global sightings.

More UFOs over Warminster

Arthur Shuttlewood

London: Arthur Baker, 1979

Shuttlewood's last book, it is a reworking of chapters from earlier books, and mainly concerned with revisiting the sightings that had defined the mystery.

The Warminster Triangle

Ken Rogers

Warminster: Coates and Parker, 1994

This was the first book post-Shuttlewood to revisit the Warminster mystery. Following the model of Shuttlewood's books, it lists of UFO sightings, tales of paranormal activity, descriptions of historical forteana, and briefly mentions the new-fangled crop circles.

Books Relating to the Mystery

Current

Flying Saucerers

David Clarke and Andy Roberts

Loughborough, UK: Alternative Albion, 2007

A social history and history of ideas that reveals how the notions of a few inspired 'experts' evolved into one of the most pervasive modern day myths. Roberts and Clarke devote a chapter of their book to Warminster.

Zones of Strangeness: An Examination of Paranormal and UFO Hotspots

Peter A. McCue

AuthorHouse UK, 2012

Investigates the notion that certain areas "play host to a disproportionate number of paranormal events". Can reports from such areas can be believed, and if so, are the phenomena genuinely paranormal and are such areas really the centres of unusually high numbers of anomalous events? Contains a chapter about the Warminster mystery.

Out of Print

The Scoriton Mystery

Eileen Buckle

HB: London: Neville Spearman, 1967
PB: London: New English Library, 1979

Contains a chapter entitled "A Week in Warminster". Buckle, Philip Rodgers and Norman Oliver visited the town as part of their investigation into the events that occurred in Scoriton, Devon, in April 1965. During their stay, they visited Cradle Hill and took part in a sky-watch. Among the participants was Arthur Shuttle-wood.

Flying Saucers are Hostile

Brad Steiger and Joan Whritenour

PB: New York: Award Books, 1967; London: Tandem, 1967 (repr. 1970, 1972, 1975)

Steiger has written numerous books on UFOs and the paranormal. The title of this somewhat racy tome says it all. A chapter describes events also reported in *The Warminster Mystery*, but we feel that these have been jazzed up.

Unidentified Flying Objects

Robert Chapman

HB: London: Arthur Baker, 1969
PB: London: Mayflower/Fontana, 1975-1981

Chapter Five, "Why Warminster?", recaps the events in Warminster up until late 1968. Robert Chapman, who, at the time, was the Science Correspondent at the Sunday

Express, visited Cradle Hill with Shuttlewood as part of his research into his book.

Can You Speak Venusian

Patrick Moore

HB: London: David & Charles, 1972
PB: London: Mayflower/Fontana, 1976,

An entertaining romp around the fringes of science with various free-thinkers. The chapter *Crockery from the Void* concentrates mainly on his visit to Warminster and conversations with Arthur Shuttlewood.

UFO-UK

Peter Paget, London: NEL Books, 1980

Various UFO cases from Warminster are mentioned in passing throughout the book, but a chapter provides details of the unusual contactee experiences of Kevin Goodman and his friends.

Appendix
The Drama of the First Year

This appendix provides a list and timeline of some of the events that occurred in the first year of the Warminster mystery.

Date/Time	Witness/ Location	What happened
25/12/1964 time u/k	Soldiers at Knook Camp, Heytesbury	"As if a huge chimney stack from the main block was ripped from the rooftop, then scattered in solid chunks of masonry across the whole camp area."
1.25am	Mildred Head, Warminster	"Ceiling came alive with strange sounds that lashed our roof... as if twigs were brushing the tiles... h a noise [like] giant hailstones."
6.12am	Marjorie Bye, Christ Church, Warminster	A "sonic deluge broke with full fury on an ordinary housewife.... Weirdly crackling noises... menacing sound... vibrations... Shockwaves of violent force..."

Date/Time	Witness/ Location	What happened
c. 6am	Roger Rump, Warminster	"Pounding on the roof of his home...a terrific clatter... scrambling sound..."
??/02/1965 time u/k	David Holton (and others) Crockerton, nr Warminster	"A flock of pigeons was killed in flight when tangling with the Thing. They brushed into fatal contact with paralyzing sound beams in woods in Crockerton, near Warminster... Stiff-winged, they plummeted earthward... The Thing in its most stunning guise was directly responsible... a number of people testified to a high-pitched droning..."
17/03/1965 time u/k	Joan Brown, Warminster	"...witness[ed] quivering of their roof under an onrush of noise... Their... cat... was sick in various rooms of the house that night after soundwaves dwindled."
25/03/1965 time u/k "early morning"	Ted and Gwen Davies Crockerton	"the flapping of myriad birds' wings, rustling over the rooftop, crackling round the chimney. Then came the grinding, metallic undertone... 'Our rafters shook and our windows rattled.... We thought all the birds... were migrating.'"

Date/Time	Witness/ Location	What happened
28/03/1965 11pm	Eric Payne, nr. Bishopstrow	"A whistling noise… developed into a loud buzzing... Flattened treetops on either side of me... a tremendous racket overhead. It sent shivers up my spine... "
??/05/1965 time u/k	Mrs Haines, Warminster	"Rooftop was besieged by the furious frolics of the Thing. [She] sat up in bed, face ashen, heart pounding swiftly until the… soundwaves swished to silence."
19/05/1965 time u/k	Hilda Hebdidge, Warminster	"…on three separate occasions during that week she saw unusual objects in the sky. She first related these to Barry Woodgate of the Fleet Street UFO Group... The objects were cigar-shaped and 'covered with bright lights which winked and blinked... They were various shades of gold and yellow..." *Note: Two of the objects appeared to be over Longleat, the other over Heytesbury.*
03/06/1965 8.30pm	Patricia Phillips and family, Heytesbury	"The cigar-shaped glow... hung, a brilliant spectacle in the sky for a good twenty five minutes or more… it did not

Date/Time	Witness/ Location	What happened
		change position at all. There was a distinct dark circular patch or aperture at the base of the fiery object, which threw off a halo of red-orange light. The craft was horizontal, not vertical..."
	Harold and Dora Horlock, Warminster	"Twin red-hot pokers hanging downwards, one on top of the other, with a black space in between."
	Seventeen people at Shearwater (south of Warminster)	"Seventeen people were either fishing or bathing [at] Shearwater... Crockerton. All witnessed the cigar-bodied extravaganza. 'It was obviously huge but high up,' said ... Colin Hampton, so surprised he fell into the lake. Some thought it to be orange-mauve...others... orange-red. Apart from these slight colour variations... the main descriptions agreed with [Mrs Phillips]."
12/06/1965		*News of the World* article, about the UFO seen on 9/06/65, is published. The article was written by Shuttlewood.

Date/Time	Witness/ Location	What happened
19/06/1965 8.35pm	Kathleen Penton, Warminster	Fantastic spectacle... shining Thing going sideways... Porthole type windows... To my eyes it was the size of... a bedroom wall... Windows were lit up...
25/06/1965		Letter to *Warminster Journal*. Gordon Creighton writes: "It is evident that a good deal of nonsense is being talked by some of your correspondents – and the only person who is on the right track with his thinking about the matter is David Holton."
07/07/1965 3.15am	Dora Horlock, Warminster	...a large red ball in the south which rose into the sky and hung down, opening up once more into a flaming poker. It had a black base at its rim... [It] was the size of our front room to my eyes – it was so close... A sizzling or crackling sound, not unlike eggs and bacon frying in a pan, could be heard...
10/08/1965 3.45am	Rachel Atwill, Warminster	...woken by a terrible droning sound. It made the bed and floor shake. I went over to the bedroom window and looked out... about 200 yards above

Date/Time	Witness/ Location	What happened
		the range of hills... was a bright object like a massive star... domed on top and huge in size, an unwinking light of uncanny brilliance.
4.36am	Terry Pell, Warminster	Was driving his lorry from Spalding to Warminster. With him in the cab were his wife and daughter, who were asleep. Passing Colloway Clump, a crimson light flew from the hillside on his left and hovered fifty yards in front of him, and then sped head-on towards his lorry: 'Its speed and change of direction were almost unbelievable.' Mr Pell braked sharply to avoid the UFO, but the UFO itself stopped just in front of the lorry and then proceeded to move backwards at the same speed as the lorry. His last sight of the UFO was over the Clump where it hovered for a few seconds before vanishing.
29/08/1965 time u/k (evening)	Gordon Faulkner, Warminster	"... shut the door behind him and was suddenly aware of the Thing. 'As it flew fast and low over the south of the town I could just make out the unususal shape. It made no

Date/Time	Witness/ Location	What happened
		noise. Hurriedly, I got my camera free…I did not dream I would get anything on film… and I was amazed when I saw what came out."'
10/09/1965		Both the *Warminster Journal* and *Daily Mirror* print the Faulkner photo and accompanying story. The article in the *Daily Mirror* is more detailed, and both the article and photograph are given a double page spread.
06/11/1965 9.57pm	Hilda Hebdidge, Warminster	Saw a similar object [to that she saw in May–see above] over Cop Heap..."The Thing sparkling behind the boughs".

Direct quotations are taken from the early chapters of *The Warminster Mystery*, where detailed descriptions of these sightings can be found.

Index

T

U

Also Available

In Alien Heat: The Warminster Mystery Revisited

Steve Dewey and John Ries

San Antonio and New York: Anomalist Books

ISBN-10: 1933665025
ISBN-13: 978-1933665023

The UFO fever that gripped the British town of Warminster for about a decade is now largely forgotten. It was one of the largest UFO flaps ever to occur.

The authors were themselves among the many skywatchers around Warminster and spent many nights on Cradle Hill, the centre of the phenomenon, watching and waiting for UFOs – but also watching and listening to the witnesses and UFOlogists.

This book introduces the Warminster mystery to a new generation of readers. It contains a short history of the phenomenon, places it in its social and historical context, and examines the possible mechanisms that initiated and sustained this remarkable UFO flap.

UFO Warminster: Cradle of Contact

Kevin Goodman and Steve Dewey

Fortean Words, 2012

ISBN-10: 190572392X
ISBN-13: 978-1905723928

The author and his group of friends, excited by what they had heard about the town, began to visit Warminster during the mid-1970s.

They went to there to research the UFO sightings.

But soon, they were to become the focus of the very phenomena they were researching.

This is their story.

Printed in Great Britain
by Amazon